the shepherd of the stars

the shepherd of the stars

Charles A. Trentham

BROADMAN PRESS
Nashville, Tennessee

Nashville, Tennessee

421-06255

Library of Congress catalog card number: 62-9200

Printed in the United States of America
5.S6113

This volume is humbly dedicated
to the three greatest servants of Christ
God has given me to know:
W. T. Conner
the teacher
James S. Stewart
the preacher
F. F. Brown
the pastor

Preface

At a meeting at Star Island in August, 1955, a committee on science and religion, after thorough study, decided that religion is man's effort to orient himself in his total environment. The role of religion in every age is to bring the revelation of God into focus that it may minister to the immediate needs of men.

The past decade has ushered us into a strange new world of outer space. This lays upon the Christian church the responsibility of interpreting Christianity for our new age. Most of us recoil from the catastrophic changes which lie before us. We would be quite content with the position of the foremost historian of our time, Dr. Arnold Toynbee, when he reminds us that in the face of our frantic concern to explore outer space the big problems are on this planet, not in outer space. Then he reminds us that there is not much time to put this planet in order. The farther we move into our new age, however, the more we conform to the thinking of Walt Whitman: "I was thinking this globe enough till there sprang out so noiseless around me myriads of other globes."

Mankind has been concerned with space and with sending objects into space for many centuries. The rocket was invented by the Chinese around A.D. 1200 and was first employed against the Mongols in the siege of Kaifeng in A.D. 1232. That which is new and which vitally concerns us now is the staggering truth that in the last decade the size of rockets has increased enormously. We are no longer indulging in fancy when we read Lewis Carroll's delightful lines: "Up above the world you fly, Like a tea-tray in the sky."

We now think of hurling entire planets into the heavens. Moreover, in the last decade, speeds have increased more than fivefold. These whimsical lines, quoted by Arthur C. Clarke in *The Exploration of Space,* become less humorous:

> There was a young lady named Bright
> Whose speed was far greater than light
> She set out one day
> In a relative way
> And returned on the previous night.

Our literature has long abounded in speculation concerning the heavens. Think of these passages from Fitzgerald, Pope, and Tennyson:

> Up from Earth's Centre; through the Seventh Gate
> I rose, and on the Throne of Saturn sate.

> Observe how system into system runs,
> What other planets circle other suns,
> What varied being peoples every star . . .

> Hesper—Venus—were we native to that splendor
> or in Mars,
> We should see the globe we groan in, fairest of
> their evening stars.

> Could we dream of wars and carnage, craft and
> madness, lust and spite,
> Roaring London, raving Paris, in that point of
> peaceful light?

Yet only in our decade have we had to face realistically the prospect of traveling out beyond the gravitational pull of the earth. For the great venture which lies before us we must ask, "Are thy wings plumed indeed for such far flights?" Religion's role is to prepare us for the flight and to help answer the paramount question, as phrased by Whitman, "Ah, who shall soothe these feverish children? Who justify these restless explorations?"

What I have attempted here is, first of all, to discuss the relevance of the Colossian letter to our immediate spiritual problems. I have traced the similarity between the conditions of our age and of the age in which the Colossian Christians lived. I have shown that theirs also was an age of crisis, an age when the world was shrinking, drawing mankind closer together; and an age when Christianity was in the death struggle with those who would consider her as only one among the many religions of mankind. The three major threats to the original gospel which converged on the congregation at Colossae will be identified as a pagan cosmology, philosophism, and syncretism, or the endeavor to subject Christianity to a minor role in a composite gospel. I shall also endeavor to point the way toward a theology of space and a Christian cosmology as they arise out of the Colossian letter. Part 2 is composed of twenty-eight brief expositions from Colossians as they were preached at the First Baptist Church, Knoxville, Tennessee, in the summer of 1960.

The title THE SHEPHERD OF THE STARS was chosen because only a Christ who holds the seven stars in his hands (Rev. 1:16) is adequate to stabilize our souls in this age of space. Only the Christ who is the perfect embodiment of the God of whom the psalmist sang: "He healeth the broken in heart, and bindeth up their wounds. He telleth the number of the stars; he calleth them all by their names" (Psalm 147:3-4) is adequate for our age of space. James Stewart once said, "Only a star-counting God can deal with the complexities of our times."

Eleven years ago I began the serious study of the Colossian epistle. While attending the lectures of Dr. James S. Stewart at New College in the University of Edinburgh, my interest in this epistle was first kindled. To Dr. Stewart I owe an immeasurable debt of gratitude.

Believing that this epistle presents a vivid picture of Christianity in conflict with some of the various religions and philosophies which sought to undermine the Christian gospel in the first century, I offered a course in the theology of Colossians for several years at Southwestern Baptist Theological Seminary, in Fort Worth, Texas. Some of this material I included in the theological lectures at Golden Gate Baptist Theological Seminary, Berkeley, California, in the winter of 1958.

My thanks are due and are gratefully given to all who have heard these lectures and have encouraged their printing. My thanks also are offered to my secretary, Mary Elizabeth Tyler, who has often gone the second mile in typing an illegible morass of material.

Contents

Part One
INTRODUCTION

1. The Relevance of the Colossian Letter

A staggering proportion of our national budget is being spent to explore untraveled space; and we are hurling astronauts into realms where a few years ago man never dared to dream of going, except after his spirit left his body at death. We are being told that within ten years, if our earthly civilization survives, we shall build a civilization on the moon. Such facts and predictions lay upon us the necessity of reaffirming the adequacy of the Christian gospel for our age. We soon must determine whether or not the best within us transcends even that which is highest among the stars.

Describing dimensions of the universe which man is endeavoring now to explore, Cecilia Payne-Gaposchkin, the Phillips astronomer of Harvard University, reminds us that the unaided eye of man can see about five thousand stars. With the assistance of a four-inch lens he may see over two million, and with the two-hundred-inch mirror over a billion stars may be seen.[1] A visit to Mount Palomar affords an opportunity to look through telecopes which reveal that our own galaxy is composed of probably one hundred billion stars and that there are millions of other galaxies spaced about one million light-years apart. (One light-year is approximately six trillion miles.)

With such astronomical dimensions before us, do you wonder that ancient man once believed that lunacy was induced by contemplating the heavenly bodies? In the presence of such vast reaches of space some have reasoned that it would be the rankest form of extravagance if life were found only on this fragment of dust floating through the ether which we call earth. Still others remind us that extravagance must be measured in terms of what we know God has done and not in terms of what our finite minds imagine he should have done.

Harlow Shapley speculates that there are at least ten million billion planetary sites where life might go on. Furthermore, he affirms that the evidence is strong, though not yet conclusive, that there is life on Mars. Writing of the frequency of life-bearing planets, Harlow Shapley tells us:

> In a speculative frame of mind let's say that only one in a hundred is a single star, and of them only one in a hundred has a system of planets, and of them only one in a hundred has an earthlike planet, and of them only one in a hundred has its earth in that interval of distance from the star that we call the liquid-water-belt (neither too cold nor too hot), and of them only one in a hundred has the chemistry of air, water, and land something like ours—suppose all those chances were approximately true, then we would find a planet suitable for biological experiment for only one star in ten billion. But there are so many stars! We would still have ten billion planets suitable for organic life something like that on the earth.
>
> In the opinion of most scientists who have pondered this situation in recent years, I have here greatly underestimated the frequency of good planetary sites for biology; we should increase the number by a million times at least, increase it to ten million billion.[2]

On July 23, 1960, a news release from London declared that British astronomers had discovered a new galaxy of stars farther out into space than man had ever seen before. The star system, resembling the Milky Way, is thirty-six quadrillion miles away from the earth. It takes five billion light-years to reach the earth from the newly found stars, called only Galaxy 3C-295.

"In other words, we are seeing a sample of the universe as it was all those millions of years ago," said Professor Martin Ryle of the Mullard Radio Astronomy Laboratory at Cambridge University, when he lectured at Britain's Royal Society on July 23, 1960.

When a man makes it to the moon, he has not taken an infant's step on his journey through the vast reaches of space. In this decade of destiny we are once more confronted with the question of the adequacy of the simple religion of the man of Nazareth and the Christ of Galilee. Must our Christian faith undergo major alterations in the light of fresh, unfolding scientific truth of which the apostles never dreamed? We are told we must "carry from the altar of the past the fire not the ashes."[3]

The question immediately before us is whether or not we have in the living Christ an adequate religion to match our modern cosmology, to sustain the twentieth-century mind as well as the immortal soul. May we, in the light of our new discoveries, still affirm that when man has met Christ as his Redeemer, he can then see him as his creator and sing with the poet Joseph Addison:

> The spacious firmament on high,
> With all the blue ethereal sky,
> And spangled heavens, a shining frame,
> Their great Original proclaim.
> The unwearied Sun, from day to day,
> Does his Creator's power display;
> And publishes, to every land
> The work of an Almighty hand.
>
> Soon as the evening shades prevail,
> The Moon takes up the wondrous tale;
> And nightly to the listening Earth

Repeats the story of her birth:
Whilst all the stars that round her burn,
And all the planets in their turn,
Confirm the tidings as they roll
And spread the truth from pole to pole.

What though, in solemn silence, all
Move round the dark terresterial ball?
What though nor real voice nor sound
Amidst their radiant orbs be found?
In Reason's ear they all rejoice,
And utter forth a glorious voice;
For ever singing as they shine,
"The Hand that made us is divine."

By stretching our electronic techniques to the utmost, we may now get a readable Morse signal to the nearest star. When we are able to establish satellite listening posts above the electrical interference of earth, we may then search for intelligently modulated signals from space and determine the existence of extraterrestrial intelligences.

Our species has appeared only in the last five-thousandth of earth's history, while the total length of human civilization spans barely a millionth of that time. Since our species is so relatively young when measured by the total age of the earth, some have speculated that if there are extraterrestrial creatures, they must be superior to us by many millions of years of growth and development.

It is then most relevant that we should ask if there be anything in the untraveled spheres which will upset our faith. The answer must be an answer of faith and it is found in one of the smallest and most insignificant of the first-century churches, the church at Colossae. One of the amazing characteristics of the Christian Scriptures is that always they have yielded new light to meet every new demand.

Of the great apostle's writings, the Colossian epistle is perhaps the most relevant for our decade. It deals with three major and immediate concerns which strangely parallel our own.

A Crisis Theology

First of all, Colossians contains a crisis theology. We who live in such perilous days, when civilization hangs moment by moment in the balance, when our entire planet may be consumed by thermonuclear war, may profit greatly by reading a letter written to a church in a city which literally lived on the edge of a volcano. It is believed that only a few months after Paul wrote this letter, the entire city was blown into oblivion by a cataclysmic earthquake during the reign of Nero (A.D. 60 or 61).[4]

A Shrinking World

In the second place, this epistle should hold our interest because it was written during a period when the world was drawing nearer together. Men's eyes were being opened to wider horizons. The meteoric career of Alexander the Great had completed the dissolution of the social structure so that life no longer moved around the pivot of the city states of the Greek world and the empire states of the Orient. No longer was man pondering primarily his relationship with his immediate society. One of his chief concerns was to interpret his relationship to his universe and to realize that men must learn to live together on this earth or they cannot live on this earth at all. Even so, today, after the military forces in two wars have shattered our nationalistic barriers and the powers of science have penetrated into outer space, the horizons of our theology must be lifted, as we say again with S. W. Foss the poet:

> As wider skies broke on his view,
> God greatened in his growing mind;
> Each year he dreamed his God anew,
> And left his older God behind.

He saw the boundless scheme dilate,
In star and blossom, sky and clod;
And as the universe grew great,
He dreamed for it a greater God.

Christianity in Conflict

Our paramount interest in this epistle lies in the fact that it describes the conflict between Christianity and many of the pagan cults which the heralds of the cross encountered in the Hellenistic culture of the first century.

Although now desolate, the region in which Colossae stood was once one of the wealthiest and most populous areas of the east. The three cities in the valley were Colossae, Laodicea, and Hierapolis. Although Colossae was the smallest of the cities, it was the oldest. Indeed, it was an ancient city when Xenophon passed through on his memorable march and is mentioned by Herodotus as a palace of great importance. Colossae knew such important guests as Xerxes in 481 B.C. and Cyrus the Younger in 401 B.C.[5]

Colossae lay in the Lycus Valley on the main trade route from the Euphrates River on the east to the great city of Ephesus and the Aegean Sea on the west. Over this road traveled every form of philosophy and religion in the ancient world.

The population of Colossae was composed largely of Phrygians with a Greek admixture. We know that nearby Laodicea had a large Jewish population and it is probable that this was also true of Colossae. It is, therefore, very probable that the membership of the Colossian congregation was composed of Phrygians, Greeks, and Jews and that they brought into this church diverse backgrounds of religious thought and experience.

Speculation Concerning Space

The religion of the ancient world included a strange theology of the heavens. We are not in any wise to think that our concern with the heavens is exclusively modern. Two thousand years ago

Hipparchus made a record of the same constellations which still look down upon us in the night. Homer was as familiar with the Dipper and Orion as we are. The ancient Babylonians described the highway along which the sun journeys among the stars, which we call the zodiac. The Milky Way, the great river of stars, was just as familiar to the ancient man as to us, and so was Orion, the blazing hunter who climbed up over the eastern horizon, followed by Sirius, his faithful dog star.

The majesty and mystery of the stars filled the nights with magic. You do not wonder then that astrology was the queen of the sciences. Even the Roman emperors, such as Julius Caesar and Augustus, would never make important decisions without consulting the stars. Alexander the Great believed that his fate was fixed by the stars.

This belief gave rise to wild and unbridled speculation concerning the inhabitants of space. Men of the first century believed with Pythagoras that the whole air was full of spirits. Philo, the Alexandrian scholar, also felt that there were spirits flying everywhere through the air and that the air was the house of disembodied spirits. In the days of Paul, men believed very strenuously in demons. To them the air was so crowded with these demons that it was impossible to move anywhere through space without encountering them.

The Jews also added their thoughts of the heavens to that of the ethnic world. We know that when Abraham left Ur of the Chaldees, even then the people were worshiping the moon. The excavations of Woolley at Ur has fairly well established that Ur and Haran were both great centers of worship of Nannar, the moon goddess. A temple to the moon goddess has been found at Mari, which lay midway on the route from Ur to Haran. The Old Testament writers appear in places to think of the stars as personal beings. In Nehemiah 9:6, the prophet sees the host of heaven worshiping God (cf. Isa. 24:21,23). In the song of Deborah stars are seen fighting against Sisera (Judg. 5:20). The morning stars are identified with the sons of God (Job 38:7). In the pseudepigrapha, Enoch 18:14 tells of "a prison for the stars of heaven and the host of heaven," and also of "the stars which have transgressed the commandment of God and are bound here till 10,000 ages, the number of days of their guilt, are consummated."

In the Septuagint (Deut. 4:19) the nations are assigned to the host of heaven, or the sons of God, while Yahweh chooses Israel for himself. Also in the Wisdom literature this is found (Sirach 17:17). In Deuteronomy the nations are described as having their angels, while Israel has Yahweh; yet when Daniel wrote, Israel also is assigned an angel. Michael and the hosts of the high ones are connected with the kings of the earth (Dan. 12:1).

It is impossible to harmonize these ancient beliefs or to say for certain what the members of the Colossian church believed on the subject. We do know, however, that the people of Colossae worshiped angels and that Michael was regarded as the protector of the city. It was said that he once appeared to the people saving the city in a time of flood.[6]

To know what the Colossians believed about the inhabitants of space can only be deduced from those passages in which Paul offers his gospel as a corrective to pagan speculation concerning the heavenlies. To understand those passages it is helpful to remember how Paul writes in other letters. In Galatians, Paul sees the angels as connected with nature. He describes them as "the elements of the world" (Gal. 4:3,9), which he regards as the personal elemental world to which this world was in subjection. When Paul speaks of the "celestial bodies" (1 Cor. 15:40), he is probably seeing the stars as animated bodies.

For Paul not even the angels were morally perfect. He sees certain angels, principalities, and powers which threaten to separate us from the love of God (Rom. 8:38-39). He refers to an angel which may preach a different doctrine from his own (Gal.

1:8). He sees the principalities and powers brought under subjection to Christ (1 Cor. 15:24). The rulers of this world, through ignorance, were responsible for the crucifixion of the Lord of glory (1 Cor. 2:6-8). He sees Christians judging the angels (1 Cor. 6:3). Paul also recognized ranks of angels (Rom. 8:38). In 1 Thessalonians 4:16, he mentions the archangel. In Galatians 3:19, he sees the law as given through the mediation of angels.

The adoration of angels was a common practice among the Jews. Twice in Revelation the angel who reveals the visions to the writer also urges him to refrain from worshiping him (Rev. 19:10; 22:8-9). Paul saw Christ triumphing over the angels, for by his death on the cross he abolished the law which had been mediated by the angels (Col. 2:15).

Despite Paul's insistence that Christ created all things visible and invisible (Col. 1:16), which would include the angelic orders, and that the angels are subject to Christ, angel worship continued even into the Middle Ages. This is seen in the fact that the Council of Laodicea, convening about the middle of the fourth century, had to condemn angel worship. In the fifth century, Theodoret tells us that the worship of Michael was still being observed.

It was the Colossians' worship of angels and their belief in strange, hostile powers in the heavenlies that called forth Paul's letter to their church (Col. 2:8,18). The Colossians were contending that the Christian gospel was adequate in the moral realm in providing redemption from sin. They insisted, however, that this was not mankind's only problem. The major problem lay in their belief that malign, hostile powers in the heavenlies were continually plotting the destruction of man. When death came, before the soul could pass into the presence of the most high God, it must pass through the spheres which were inhabited and controlled by demons. Some Colossian teachers believed that only as man possessed secret passwords, and only as these demons were placated, could he ever pass into his eternal home.

The question before the Colossian congregation was whether or not Christ has control of the heavenlies as well as the visible earth. Paul answers that all things, even the heaven of heavens and all things therein, have their existence in Christ. He is the creator, sustainer, and final goal toward which all things move (Col. 1:15-20).

Notes

1. Cecilia Payne-Gaposchkin, *Stars in the Making* (Cambridge: Harvard University Press, 1952), p. 3. By permission.
2. Harlow Shapley (ed.), *Science Ponders Religion* (New York: Appleton-Century-Crofts, Inc., 1960), p. 8. Used by permission.
3. *Ibid.,* p. 98.
4. A. S. Peake, "The Epistle to the Colossians," *The Expositor's Greek Testament,* ed., W. Robertson Nicoll (Grand Rapids: Wm. B. Eerdmans Publishing Co., n.d.), III, 477.
5. E. J. Banks, "Colossae," *The International Standard Bible Encyclopedia,* ed., James Orr *et al.* (Grand Rapids: Wm. B. Eerdmans Publishing Co., 1939), II, 676. Used by permission.
6. *Ibid.*

2. Conditions in Colossae

It was a crisp, clear night in the Lycus Valley outside the city of Colossae. The stars, the "forget-me-nots of the angels," blossomed beautifully in the garden of God. The youthful shepherd's soul was filled with reverent wonder as he watched the manifold constellations walk in majesty and beauty through the night. Many a night had he watched the passage of the stars across the night sky. He had learned to tell the time of year by the rising of some stars and the sinking of others. He had learned from older shepherds to give the names of animals to the great forms they imagined they saw the stars make—the ram, the bull, the big and little bears, the lion, and the dog.

Above the Lycus River flowed the Milky Way, the great river of stars, which was just as familiar to the shepherd during his night watch as were the green and fertile pastures along the banks of this tributary of the Maeander River. This region was noted for its great breed of sheep. Many were the shepherds who tended their flocks in this valley. The long, long thoughts of the lonely shepherd have often contributed immeasurably to humanity's religious lore. Shepherds have always been students of the stars, for in the solitary nights they came to feel that stars were their close companions. The shepherd king of Israel felt that God was the creator of the stars. He therefore called upon them to praise him: "Praise ye him, sun and moon: praise him, all ye stars of light. Praise him, ye heavens of heavens, and ye waters that be above the heavens" (Psalm 148:3-4). To David, God dwelt beyond the light of all setting suns and was the great shepherd of the stars. God alone can really see the full glory of the heavens.

> With the long shadows lying
> Black in a land alight
> With a more luminous wonder
> Than ever comes to our night.[1]

If the Colossian congregation included a cross section of humanity, as was true of most first-century churches, some of these shepherds must have been members of this church. Their mystical, vertical gaze into the heavens must have served to counterbalance the horizontal tides and pressures from all parts of the ancient world which converged on this little congregation.

Remember the time and the location of the church. It was the middle of the first Christian century, an age of travel. The church stood on the great trade route which ran from the Euphrates on the east to the great city of Ephesus, one hundred miles away on the west. The details of the origin of the church are unknown to us. We do know that Paul had never visited the church (Col. 1:4). It is thought that Epaphras (Col. 4:12), who was probably one of Paul's converts during his great ministry in Ephesus, was the founder of the church.

This little congregation stood to bear the full brunt of every attempt of ethnic philosophy and religion to destroy the Christian faith. The Colossians were familiar with the grand endeavors of the ethnic scholars to interpret God, man, and the universe. The conflict which arose between the Colossian Christians and the ethnic religions cannot rightly, however, be called a struggle between a rigidly formulated orthodox Christianity and the clearly formulated heresy; for, in truth, there was at this point (about A.D. 60) no well-defined Christian theology. Much of the New Testament had not yet been written. Paul, John, and others were still in the process of interpreting the meaning of Christ and his gospel to the church. We can discern the nature of the pagan challenge to the Christian gospel solely by reading Paul's brief refutation of this challenge.

Heretical Undercurrents

E. F. Scott contends that "to attach a particular label to the heresy may all be regarded as futile."[2] Yet, we do know that the problem which had arisen in the Colossian church was not a speculative argument over fanciful concepts of space. It was not a debate over whether or not a pinpoint could be inserted into space without touching a demon.

Paul was a magnificent controversialist, but his controversies were never over trivialities. They gathered around the grand centralities of the faith. Always they were concerned with the complete adequacy of Jesus Christ. As in the Galatian letter, he answered the Judaizers who contended that the Christian gospel needed supplementing by the Law, so now Paul answers these who contend that the worship of Christ must be supplemented by the worship of the inhabitants of space—the angels (Col. 2:18).

Pagan Cosmology

The teachers of Colossae argued that Christ was a moral Saviour of the individual and delivered all mankind from sin and its enslavement. But, said they, sin is not the only power to which man is in subjection. There are hostile, malign forces in the heavenlies which lie in wait to thwart the journey of the soul into the higher realms. These forces became so powerful that they were successful in crucifying the Lord of glory (1 Cor. 2:8). They then had to be placated by a prescribed worship, which consisted of secret rituals and passwords. The protognostic philosophers contended that they were in possession of such secret formulas which guaranteed the safe passage of the soul through the realms controlled by hostile spirits.

Paul refuted this by insisting on the solid truth that Christ is not solely the Saviour of the individual from the moral maladies of life. He is the king of the universe and of eternity by whom all things, even the ranks of angels, were created and are being sustained. Furthermore, he is the goal toward which all creation moves. Angels, therefore, are dependent upon Christ, not he on the angels. His death on the cross had liberated the Christian from all dependence upon the Law and upon angels and had bound them solely to him. No further mediators were needed.

In Colossians Paul gives us a Christian cosmology. This universe, he affirms, is not divided into warring factions presided over by spiritual forces of varying degrees of power and ability. All things are under the dominion of Christ. The Christian cosmology is grounded in the only ultimate environment which a Christian may know. He is "in Christ," the Christ in whom all the divine fulness dwells (Col. 2:9); the Christ in whom all things visible and invisible were created and toward whom, by his inexhaustible, reconciling grace, all things move.

For our age, this means that no matter how far into outer space we may venture, a Christian can never move out of Christ nor can he ever get beyond his loving care and control.

Philosophism

Another part of the problem of the Colossian church was the pagan philosophy which Paul called an empty deceit (Col. 2:8). It was a subtle form of conceit which masqueraded as a form of humility and which found expression in the worship of angels. It posed as a superior form of Christianity for the superior intellects of the church.

The subtlety of the false teachers, who propagated this doctrine, made them all the more dangerous. It was not a frontal attack but an insidious subterfuge which refused to accept the finality of the Christian faith. It insisted that Christianity should be improved by assimilating into it the best elements from paganism and Judaism. It was an incipient form of gnosticism, which insisted that those in possession of certain closely guarded secrets could thereby be liberated from the lower material world and find the higher life which is reserved only for the intellectuals and the spiritually elite.

Not only was this attitude of superiority to be found among the Gnostics, Judaism also had her share. The Pharisees with their contempt for the common man, because of his ignorance of the law, is a graphic example. Paul labels this so-called philosophy a vain deceit, an empty illusion supported only by human tradition and having the elements of the world and not Christ for its substance. Their modification of Christianity, said Paul, surrendered the true substance of the Christian gospel and carried Christianity back into an insubstantial shadowland where religion dwelt before the coming of Christ. Paul further insists that in Christ alone are hid all the treasures of wisdom and knowledge (Col. 2:3).

It is a strange truth that even the Jews had sided with the Gnostics in admitting that Jesus and his gospel were far too simple. In common they contended that God and man were infinitely removed from one another. If man is to make it up the long, long ladder that separates him from God, he must encounter and overcome the strange beings that inhabit the heavens. This he could only do by mastering the mysterious, secret knowledge, the esoteric learning and hidden passwords which they had discovered and formulated.

They held that the higher levels of religion were available only to the chosen few who possessed closely guarded secret knowledge. The Jews agreed with the Gnostics at this point; however, they insisted that this special knowledge was found exclusively in the Jewish law. Said they, the Jewish ritual and ceremonial law contain the special knowledge which enables man to ascend into the presence of God. The major difference between the Gnostics and the Jewish point of view lay in the moral realm. To the Gnostics, man's moral behavior was not so important. They concluded that the possession of this superior knowledge was the supreme concern of religion and that the ethical pattern of man's behavior was relatively unimportant.

On the other hand, the Jews lifted this question: "Who shall ascend into the hill of the Lord? or who shall stand in his holy place?" They answered by saying, "He that hath clean hands, and a pure heart; who hath not lifted up his soul unto vanity, nor sworn deceitfully" (Psalm 24:3-4). Still was it true that the Jew as well as the Gnostic endorsed a rigid exclusiveness which separated the spiritually elite from the common horde.

Paul answered both the Gnostics and the Jews by insisting on the universality of the gospel. He refuted this spiritual snobbery by declaring his purpose to warn every man and teach every man in all wisdom "that we may present every man perfect in Christ Jesus" (Col. 1:28). Paul's stress on "every man" is constantly reiterated here. The word "all" occurs twenty-nine times in this brief epistle and the word "every" six times.

The supreme concern of the Colossian mind at the time was the place of the individual in the cosmos rather than the place of the person in the social order. Man needed not merely forgiveness for his sins but reconciliation with the cosmos. Between man and the highest divinity, declared the Colossian teachers, stood a multiplicity of mediators. The totality of these angelic beings was called the *plērōma* (Col. 1:19; 2:9). These were the powers who could reconcile humanity with the cosmos.

Behind this shifting emphasis lay the fact that under Alexander the social structure of the Greek city states and the empire states of the Orient had collapsed. With the disintegration of ancient society the horizons of humanity were lifted. The old gods who presided over these communities were no longer reverenced. Man was lifted out of the context of the community into the context of the cosmos. With this the individuality of the old gods was absorbed into the concept of a universal divine power of which Zeus, Serapis, and all other gods were merely symbols.

The result was a stupendous pantheism which combined the ancient deities. So colossal was this pantheism that it seemed too vast and remote to supply adequate sympathy for the lonely soul of man. Man was not created for cold communion with the cosmos. He must have the support of other souls. He must know the undergirding of a social order. He must have a divinity who is near, who provides more solace than the vast unity of the cosmos could ever give.

In response to this demand, the gnostic schools came into being. They pretended that they were guardians of esoteric doctrines, combining elaborate systems of magic and astrology which reached back into immemorial antiquity. They claimed to be the custodians of a revelation concerning the nature of God, man, and the universe. The gnostic position then was a product of the spiritual instability of the times. What those doctrines at Colossae actually were, we can only imagine. Some believe that they may have been a form of theosophy, such as Neoplatonism, claiming to derive knowledge of God and the world by direct, mystical insight or by philosophical speculation, or by a combination of both.

The Colossian problem also contained elements of Jewish asceticism concerned with the observance of festivals, the keeping of the sabbath, and the avoidance of things unclean (Col. 2:16). These false teachers had evidently insisted that the ascetic life is a part of the discipline by which the elemental spirits were placated. They concluded that to practice asceticism one must know the rules. The Jews, in turn, claimed that they could provide the rules.

Paul answered this by saying, let no man lay down rules for you (Col. 2:16-23). The life of the Spirit cannot be defined in terms of rules. No law written by man is adequate to define the full law of God. When a man is in Christ, he has a far better guide than any rule or set of rules can ever provide. Asceticism has never lifted man's moral level, for the higher morality is not the product of severing one's self from the normal use of God's good gifts, but rather in openly repudiating all evil thoughts and actions in the midst of the crowded mart and busy streets of the world.

A Composite Gospel

Finally, the Colossian problem had to do with the attempt of Christians within the Colossian church to form a composite gospel. They attempted to blend all the supposedly superior elements of the known religions, one with another, and then to fuse these with the best of philosophy as a supplement to the Christian gospel.

This very attempt was a denial of the basic nature of the gospel as the final revelation of God to man. This attempt represented the desire of men to exploit and edit even the Christian gospel until it conformed to their own philosophy. It is not strange that such teachers should have been in the church, for all over the Empire men were at work desperately attempting to reconstruct the shattered religious systems by combining the desirable elements of all known systems into an acceptable syncretism. In Colossae the attempt was made at a heterogeneous blending of the Greek elements of religion with the Jewish elements into a hybrid faith.

Not even the Jews were immune to this endeavor, for in the world of the Diaspora they were much less restrained by the Temple cult. A pertinent example of this is in Philo of Alexandria, who reinterpreted Judaism in terms of the philosophy of Plato. He made some of the teachings of Moses to conform to the pattern of Greek philosophy.

These Jews were not newcomers to Colossae. They had been

there long enough to absorb much of the local thought into their theology. They were transported there first from Mesopotamia in 200 B.C. Their ancestors had long been under the influence of Iranian religion. The Jewish doctrine of angels, with its careful defining of classes and categories, was known first in the Iranian religion.

It was an age of religious syncretism. The Christian church at Colossae was in for a strong battle as the syncretists sought to supplement and enhance the primitive gospel. Always the question at the forefront was whether the gospel of Jesus Christ was adequate or whether it needed enlarging. The modern counterpart to this is found in the problem confronting our Christian missionaries in many lands. The question they face is whether or not we must blend Christianity with Buddhism so that we may appeal to the Chinese. Or, coming closer home, we ask, must we divest the gospel of its supernatural elements so that it may not offend the scientism which is the religion of the modern college campus?

A virile gospel must be preached on our mission fields, for the Moslem conquest is the greatest it has been since the Crusades of one thousand years ago. Abdul Nasser, the Egyptian dictator, is reported to have set 1966 as the target date for an all-Moslem black Africa. Conversion of Africa's one hundred and fifty million pagans is progressing apace, while Christian missionaries in Africa recount wholesale defections to the religion of the Star and Crescent. The Moslem taunt is that Africans are fools to hold to a religion of the white man. They even call Christ the God of white imperialism, racism, and colonialism.

Christian churches must be called out of their apathy to champion great humanitarian causes until the masses shall know that Christ does not stand on the side of oppression. Historians on both sides of the Atlantic (Brogan of Cambridge and Commager of Columbia) say that never before has the church (in the U. S.) been materially more powerful and spiritually less effective.

Often we are aroused by great spiritual insights from the entertainment world. Steve Allen, in his autobiography *Mark It and Strike It,* wrote:

> More and more in recent years I have been appalled by the fact that almost all good, constructive steps toward social justice and the brotherhood which Christ came to preach—steps such as better wages and working conditions for the laboring man, collective bargaining, old-age pensions, social security, a more democratic share in America for the Negro, better medical care for the poor, better mental health facilities for our entire society, and abolishment of the death penalty—have been characterized by their opponents as the work of Communists. If there ever was a more tragic folly, I cannot think of it.[3]

If we are not moved by this, then we should hear the words of a columnist who recently described the Communists' efforts to infiltrate every vital area of American life. He contends that it is far from accidental that communism concentrates on three areas: education, unions, and entertainment. What is shocking is that these are the areas where the Communists say ideas flourish and thinking patterns are formed. The churches are not included in the areas where ideas flourish and thought patterns are formed. How appalling that Communists are not endeavoring to infiltrate our churches because they do not feel them important enough! Could it be that we have so softened and accommodated our gospel that it has lost its magnetism? We must reaffirm the complete adequacy of the Christian gospel.

Paul answered these ancient syncretists as we must answer the modern: "Christ is all," he said. Christ is able to supply all our needs. We need nothing more! Paul did not speculate as did the ancient philosophers who debated how God, who is perfectly good, could come into contact with matter which the Greek considered evil. For him this problem had been conclusively settled in the actual historic incarnation. He had met Jesus Christ outside the gates of Damascus. This existential encounter had ushered Paul into a new universe and had given him a cosmology of his own. It was not necessary for him to harmonize his experience with the fashionable cosmology of his day.

The Christ who had disclosed himself to Paul made himself known as his Redeemer. It was not difficult for Paul to believe that the Christ who had so radically remade his soul was the Christ who made him in the beginning. Because he was in Christ, he could see Christ all around him. "If any man be in Christ, he is a new creature" (2 Cor. 5:17). Knowing Christ first as Redeemer, Paul came later to know him as the Lord of all his universe (Acts 9:1-19; 22:1-21; 26:1-23; 1 Cor. 9:1; 15:8; Gal. 1:15-16; Eph. 3:3; Phil. 3:12).

This is the fathomless metaphysic and cosmology behind Charles Wesley's hymn: "Thou, O Christ, art all I want; More than all in Thee I find." This is not the mere sentimentalism of a pious hymn. It is bedrock Christian reality.

This epistle then is concerned with the complete adequacy of Christ. It answers the question, is he among the elemental spirits which compose the pleroma (the full complement of divine beings) or does the pleroma dwell in him? Is he one among the many mediators or is he the only way to God?

Absorbed as we are today in the thoroughgoing determinism of the philosophical realm and engrossed with the power of the atom in the scientific realm, once again man is asking, do not Christ and his religion need supplementing? Does not our real security reside in physical force? Is not man actually at the mercy of blind forces beyond his control? Or is Christ's hand actually at the helm of the universe? Is our universe really grounded in Christ and controlled by him? If so, what relevance has Christ for science, economics, and government?

No higher Christology appears on the pages of our New Testament than that which Paul wrote to the Colossians. We need to understand this in our time. For here Paul gives us a Christian cosmology to match the challenge of our age of space. Here also he gives us a cosmic ethic which alone will match the demand of our day.

If Christ controls this universe, we may believe that it does not lie ultimately in man's power to set the time of its destruction. If thermonuclear war comes, civilization may be set back 250 years. Yet, when it is over, chastened men may creep out of their caves, blink their half-blinded eyes, rack their shocked and shattered minds, and start over. This will not be the end of man, for this is God's world.

Here then, I offer twenty-eight brief expositions based on a continuous exegesis of the epistle which Paul wrote from Rome to the Colossian church around the year A.D. 60.

Notes

1. Lord Dunsany, "At the Time of the Full Moon," *Fifty Poems* (London: Putnam & Co. Ltd., 1930). Used by permission.
2. E. F. Scott, "The Epistles of Paul to the Colossians, to Philemon and to the Ephesians," *The Moffatt New Testament Commentary,* ed. James Moffatt (6th ed.; New York: Harper & Brothers, n.d.), p. 7. Used by permission.
3. Steve Allen, *Mark It and Strike It* (New York: Holt, Rinehart & Winston, Inc., 1960), p. 390. Used by permission.

Part Two
EXPOSITION

3. The Hope Laid Up in Heaven

Colossians 1:1-5

The most conservative thinkers of our time, who are not in any wise given to exaggeration, readily admit that we are living in one of humanity's most ominous and epochal hours. Some rash blunder may at any moment plunge us into a war which no one can win. To add to our horror, the Soviet Union has hurled bombs halfway around the world in twenty-two minutes by intercontinental missiles.

Our thoughts turn back often to those words of Sir Edmund Grey, who said on a fateful evening in 1914, "The lights are going out all over Europe tonight and they may not come on again in our generation." We are still living in the dark aftermath and terrific tension of the fulfilment of that prophecy.

Only now is the darkness beginning to encircle our own continent. We have lived thus far in an isolated paradise. Many miles of water have separated us from all who would do us harm. But now the trouble in the Belgian Congo, the tumult in Laos, and the Cuban uprising converge to cause us to tremble, for we dwell behind a secure bulwark no longer. The trampled masses of humanity hold in contempt a fat America hoarding food in a starving world while our Communist adversary has built the only new empire of the twentieth century. In fifteen years a third of the world's population has been swept behind the iron and bamboo curtains.

What Prime Minister MacMillan said of Africa is true of us. The winds of change are blowing through this continent. Relentless racial uprisings, wars and rumors of wars are throwing their black, ominous shadows across the earth. Where can we look for hope and help?

Paul once wrote a letter to a church in circumstances very similar to our own. He wrote to a church in the heart of a city which, although they knew it not, was soon to be blown into oblivion by a cataclysmic earthquake. This then is a letter we should read and understand.

Not only was there a tumult outside this ancient church, there was also turmoil within the congregation. Certain teachers had infiltrated the congregation, teaching that the simple gospel of Jesus was all right for the unsophisticated masses but it was far too naïve for those who had known the advantages of superior training in the wisdom of the philosophers, the intelligentsia who were capable of receiving special revelation and discovering deeper insights which would lift them above the common horde of humanity.

These were not unlike our own people who delight disdainfully to speak of other churches as "people's churches" to distinguish them from the church of the elite. They called themselves Gnostics, "the knowers." They knew so little that they thought they knew it all. They pretended to possess certain secret passwords and insights into spiritual reality which lifted them high above their fellow Christians who knew only the simple gospel of the Nazarene. They were so depraved and deluded that they had the brazen effrontery to contend that they could supplement the revelation of God given in its fulness in Christ Jesus.

As is often the case, they felt that their superior knowledge atoned for their neglect of their religious duties and their moral failures. They were like those modern Christians who say, "I teach the Word of God on Sunday. This atones for my refusal to attempt to lead men to the Saviour on Monday." How can any man teach the gospel without acknowledging that it is the good news of God's grace in Christ which he must constantly make known to all men? These Gnostics were the self-appointed, chosen few who scorned the simple, straightforward faith once for all delivered to the saints. To substantiate their own opinion, they were ready to undermine the very faith on which the Christian church was founded by making it conform to the pagan philosophy of their own day.

Knowing that insidious falsehood spreads rapidly, that some will believe anything they read in print, and that the life of the church was being threatened, Epaphras, the pastor, hastened to Rome where Paul was imprisoned to seek the counsel of the great apostle. This is the letter which Paul wrote in defense of the adequacy of the simple gospel of the Redeemer.

Paul had never been to Colossae. In Colossians 1:4, he says, "Since we heard of your faith." Yet he was well known throughout this region. For it was while he was preaching at Ephesus that missionaries went into the Lycus Valley, one hundred miles due east of Ephesus, to establish the Colossian church. It was not, therefore, as A. S. Peake supposes, to make himself known to the Colossians that he calls himself an apostle.[1] He mentions his apostleship, not to inform them about himself, but to undergird the importance of what he is about to say. There was no mock humility in Paul. He never believed that Christian humility included disdaining the office to which Christ had called him. He magnified his office (Rom. 11:13), for he knew that true humility did not mean servility and timidity.

An apostle was one who was sent as the ambassador of heaven

to bear the authoritative message of heaven. An ambassador does not deliver his own message but the message of his sovereign, the king. Paul's message is not his own but the message of the king of heaven. He was God's appointed messenger to bear his gospel to the Gentiles. He did not, therefore, proclaim his message as a bit of casual advice which men, at their own discretion, might accept or reject.

He is an apostle by the will of God. No man can appoint himself to the gospel ministry; neither can he in any wise merit the calling of God. No man in the ministry can call himself a self-made man. In truth, in all the world there are only two kinds of men, men whom God has made and remade and men who are as yet unmade because they refuse to allow God to remake them.

Paul also writes in the name of Timothy. Early Christian workers often worked in teams of two. They followed the pattern of their Lord who sent the seventy forth in pairs (Luke 10:1). Timothy, whom Paul had led to the Saviour during his first missionary journey, was the great apostle's most loyal companion, with the possible exception of Luke, the beloved physician. So close were they that Paul could write in Timothy's name as well as his own. Paul calls him brother. The warmth of the Christian gospel breathes through this word *adelphos*. The highest and noblest quality any Christian may possess is brotherliness. Paul does not call Timothy a great scholar, a great preacher, nor a great teacher. Instead, he pays him the supreme tribute by calling him "our brother."

Timothy had the grace and demeanor to draw close to people. He never considered aloofness as a Christian virtue. He knew that the grandest servant of Christ was still a poor beggar trying to help other poor beggars to find the bread of heaven.

Paul addresses this letter to the saints, the dedicated people of God, and the faithful "brethren in Christ which are at Colosse" (Col. 1:2). Despite the fact that a great heresy had invaded this church, Paul still considered it an authentic church. The church has never been a body of perfect people. Always there have been errors and imperfections in her. Yet, that which makes her a church is that she is dedicated to God.

Hagiois, translated "saints," is the word that unites the Old Testament and the New Testament. It does not proclaim a pietistic idealism which endorses a holier than thou attitude. Rather does it speak of the fact that God injects his life into the world through human personality, despite all its imperfections.

Behind all history lies the pulsing energy of the Holy Spirit. Man is the medium through which the Holy Spirit gets across into life. When the Holy Spirit makes his impact, men are made holy and are dedicated to God. As a tree turning green in the springtime is a revelation of a great cosmic force at work in the world, so a life dedicated to God is the evidence that the Spirit of God has broken through on the human scene.

Holy people, or saints, are not those narrow, bigoted ascetics who propagate a shoddy, self-centered religiosity, but those people through whom God carries on his work. They are God's steadfast, reliable servants, God's family of committed men.

Paul departs from his early formula of addressing his letter to the church as a church (which he had used in 1 and 2 Thessalonians, 1 and 2 Corinthians, and Galatians). Beginning with Romans, he addresses his letters to the saints or to the consecrated people who have been called of God and set apart from the world to be the holy people of the Most High. It seems that the more Paul apprehended the truth of God, the more he came to understand that the chief concern of God is not with institutions but with people.

The church is people. The church is not a kind of vague, abstract entity; it is individual men and women and children. As the years went on, Paul began to think less and less of the church as a whole and more and more of the church as individual men and women. Howbeit, he never lost sight of the corporate aspect of human personality. And so in the end, he sends his greetings, not to a kind of abstract society called the church, but rather to the individual men and women of which the church must always be composed.

He addresses the faithful brethren, those who have not yielded to the position propagated by those who would undermine their faith. They are faithful in the sense that they are believers in Christ and steadfast defenders of their faith.

These Christians reside in Colossae, but they live in Christ. This is the real dimension of the Christian's environment. One day they will move out of Colossae, but they would never move out of Christ. They did not know it but the hope which was laid up in heaven would soon be a reality, for a few months after this letter was written the entire city was engulfed by a colossal earthquake.

For many years this city had stood. Even during the grand march of Xenophon, more than three hundred years before Christ, it had been a flourishing city. It had stood longer than our nation has been in existence, but age is no assurance of continual survival. Suddenly Colossae vanished from the earth. But the Christians in Colossae were only folded closer to the heart of God.

Wherever a Christian lives, he lives in Christ. His peace and joy are not ultimately dependent upon his earthly dwelling place. All things of earth will change, but the fact that he is in Christ will never change. Any work a Christian does is done in Christ. This places a crown of glory on the lowliest task of earth. It may be painful, unpleasant, and unrewarding; yet a Christian can labor on in good cheer for he is in Christ and whatsoever he does, he does unto him.

Notes

1. Peake, *op. cit.*, p. 495.

4. Peace That Prevents Panic

Colossians 1:2

When Paul wrote to the church at Colossae, the first wish he voiced for them was that "grace . . . and peace, from God our Father and the Lord Jesus Christ" (Col. 1:2) might be theirs. Paul was not simply combining the casual Greek greeting of grace with the Oriental greeting of peace. When a man is wholly given to Christ, as was Paul, every word he speaks is spoken in a Christian context.

Grace for Paul was the constant outflow of God's marvelous unmerited favor. Peace was the result of God's reconciling power. It is peace which results from the divine initiative to reconcile man unto Christ and through Christ to bind all men together as strong brothers in the family of God.

No more beautiful word appears in the Greek language than the word we translate peace. It is the word from which we get the lovely lady's name Irene. Years ago while traveling in a crowded bus across the desert country of Palestine, the driver turned on the radio. I expected to hear weird eastern music. Instead, to my amazement, there blared forth the familiar strains of the American song "Good Night, Irene." It was a great favorite in the Middle East, possibly because of the beauty of the name Irene.

The human heart has always longed for peace, for a heart

at rest. We talk about peace more than any other subject. Yet the heart of humanity is caught in that strange contradiction of always longing for peace while engaging in conflict. We want peace, but we are not interested enough to pay the price for peace. The peace we want is the peace of the central calm that shelters us in the heart of the storm and keeps us uncommitted to the struggle for peace.

Conflict is always more interesting to us than peace. Even in the church there are those who apparently thrive on discord. There are always more people at a prize fight than at a prayer meeting.

Now, the great question is, how may we find the peace that prevents panic? Look first at some futile attempts to find peace.

Some tell us we will find peace through fleeing from an irritating or depressing environment. With the psalmist they cry, "Oh that I had wings like a dove! for then would I fly away, and be at rest" (Psalm 55:6). Yet our problems are not always in our environment. Most often they are within us. They are the result of the divided heart, the inner struggle between right and wrong, the attempt to soothe a sensitive conscience, and the refusal to surrender our self-centered lives to the will of God. We can never settle this conflict by fleeing from it, for wherever we go we have to take ourselves with us.

We may do as the harassed businessman who becomes so discouraged with his overwhelming responsibilities that he locks the door to his office, walks away from it, and goes out for a game of golf. The only trouble is he always has to come back to his office.

The man who drinks to escape from reality is often in the same category. The trouble is there is always the morning after. Always he must come back to himself, to the jangled nerves, the tormented conscience, the haunting sense of guilt and failure, and the dismal mood of dark depression.

Peace is not found by escape from the hard realities of life. Neither is it found by closing our eyes to the truth. Voices everywhere call us to ignore life's rougher edge and it will smooth away. Refuse to admit the reality of the unpleasant side of life, they say. Nothing is really hard except as our thinking makes it so.

Over against this stands the solid law of life, that if one has a malignancy and ignores it, the day will surely come when it can no longer be cured. Even so, if you ignore your problem, the day will come when it can no longer be solved. Evasion only drives the problem more deeply into the soul and invites the certain day of reckoning.

Others seek peace through compromise, and they find it; but it is the peace of death. The only people who do not die before they die are those who sustain their ideals in an imperfect world.

The surest and wisest way to find peace is to ask others who have found it. Of course, advice is no good unless the giver has the right to give it, unless it comes from one who has experienced what it is to be tortured in body and tormented in soul and to finally find peace.

Nothing makes a poor person more furious than to hear a rich man, who has never felt the pangs of poverty, talk about the advantages of being poor. And what can be more exasperating than to listen to some robust man stand by your hospital bed of pain and nonchalantly say, "If I were in your condition, I would do thus and so," while you, in good grace, are resisting the temptation to invite him out of your room.

No man can offer helpful advice to the suffering unless he has suffered, unless he has been so oppressed by pain and tortured with searing agony or haunted by nagging nausea which he feels he can bear no longer.

Here is a man who is qualified to give advice. He is an old man, old before his time. He has bared his breast to many a hard battle for Christ. He bears the marks of his sufferings. He has been ground beneath the heavy heel of the persecuting power of Rome. He can even hear the booming of life's sunset guns.

Paul had lived long enough to know that when Rome set her lance, she usually brought blood; and her lance had been set against him. He is now in his prison cell as one who has known many lonely ways and many darksome hours. Yet he has discovered the path to peace.

Here it is: "Let your moderation be known unto all men. The Lord is at hand. Be careful for nothing; but in every thing by prayer and supplication with thanksgiving let your requests be made known unto God. And the peace of God, which passeth all understanding, shall keep your hearts and minds through Christ Jesus" (Phil. 4:5-7).

First, let your moderation, your unbreakable, implacable forbearance and Christian consistency be made known to all men. The consistent life which bears witness to the world of the adequacy of Christ brings its treasures of peace into the soul.

"The Lord is at hand." It is easier to be good if Jesus is near. The presence of Christ brings peace to his own. When Jesus said, "My peace I give unto you: not as the world giveth, give I unto you" (John 14:27), he meant a peace which survives because he is spiritually present to nurture it. Some talk so much about his second coming that they forget the reality of his living presence. Yet, his second coming is a basic part of the gospel. "The Lord is at hand" may mean his final coming in glorious majesty to vindicate his own against all their adversaries.

"Be careful for nothing; but in every thing by prayer." Paul is not counseling an indifferent attitude toward one's responsibilities in life. Paul says that those who are careful about nothing are prayerful about everything.

"With thanksgiving" means you cannot be preoccupied with God's goodness and your own self-centeredness at the same time.

"The peace of God" is as a soldier standing guard over your heart. Have you ever felt the reassurance of the message on the billboard along the highway: Sleep well tonight. Your National

Guard is awake. Even so, God's peace garrisons our souls. The peace of God is also peace with God, for righteousness must always precede peace. Peace with God must also issue in peace with our fellow men.

Outer peace is symptomatic of inner peace, the peace of forgiveness, the peace of confidence in the mercy of God. It is the peace of those who are in Christ. "He is our peace" (Eph. 2:14). Paul is talking about a heart at rest. "Be careful for nothing." How? Through the sentry that walks guard outside the gates of your soul. Martin Luther said that man's heart is like two grindstones. If nothing is between them, they grind on each other. Only Christ can stand between the grinding tensions of the human heart. Only through surrender to him can you ever know his peace.

> With eager heart and will on fire,
> I strove to win my great desire.
> "Peace shall be mine," I said; but life
> Grew bitter in the barren strife.
>
> . . . .
>
> Broken at last, I bowed my head,
> Forgetting all myself, and said,
> "Whatever comes, His will be done;"
> And in that moment peace was won.[1]

Notes

1. Henry van Dyke, "Peace," *The Poems of Henry van Dyke* (New York: Charles Scribner's Sons, 1924), p. 225.

5. Thoughts Which Made Paul Thankful

Colossians 1:3

The Christian church would have died in her infancy had not God called and prepared wise men to lead her through the strife and discord which often arise even among Christian people. Such a man was Paul.

When Epaphras, the pastor at Colossae, came to Rome bearing tidings of the troublemakers in the Colossian church, Paul was ready to meet it—not with a belligerent, frontal attack which might clearly express the truth but at the same time destroy the spirit of love and Christian affection in the church. He knew that truth and love move along together. To be a defender of truth does not give one a license to be an arrogant brawler. He was not so obsessed with the problem of the church that he became blind to all the good qualities in the congregation.

He does not, then, open his letter with harsh words of strong condemnation. Rather does he magnify what is right with the church he is earnestly seeking to help. So often the crusader is more intent upon vindicating his judgment than he is upon helping people.

Paul knew that he could serve the purpose of the God of love and spread the gospel of love only by "speaking the truth in love" (Eph. 4:15). To allow acrimony to be introduced into a discussion on Christian matters is in itself more heretical than any erroneous statement of doctrine can be. Truth can be learned if the spirit is kept sweet.

Paul was not always seeking for something which he could condemn in the church but for something for which he could thank God. He said, "We *always* thank God." He was not a cold, calculating politician who used even his thanks to manipulate others into feeling kindly toward him. His gratitude was a spontaneous outflow of a soul whose supreme desire was to see men committed to Christ. And when he saw this, warm feelings of thankfulness came over him. Those who knew him best contended that D. L. Moody would never sit even in a barber chair for twenty minutes without making the barber aware of his compassionate concern for him as a person and as a candidate for the kingdom of God.

We ought never to think of our church without giving genuine thanks for her. Remember that while the church has many critics, she still has no rivals. Before we were born the church gave our parents ideals of life and love which made our homes places of strength and beauty.

A character in a modern novel says: "I went to Church with my mother as a kid. I shall be buried by the Church; in between I am dashed if I scoff at the Church."[1] Henry Ward Beecher once said that the church is not a gallery for the exhibition of eminent Christians but a school for the education of imperfect ones.

"The chief trouble with the church," said Emory B. Hunt, president of Bucknell University, "is that you and I are in it."

Not that there is not much to criticize in the church. A modern youth said to his minister: "You say I am looking for something in which to have faith. It is true. I and millions like me. But ask yourself, if you will, why it is that we refuse to find a focus for our faith in your church. It is because your church has shown no understanding of the horrible morass in which we common people wade. So your churches are empty while we go in our millions to your theaters and football games. Why? Because, by my soul, those things, warped and poor as they are, are nearer to God and the common man's need for him than your church with its timid fears.

"Your church has been cowardly and lived in terror for generations. All the multiple and beautiful teachings of Christ you have thrown away because you knew they would offend the rich and privileged. To atone for your weakness, you have placed into the church of Christ the lovely trappings of art, the pomp and ceremony which Jesus never knew and could never love. Cast them out! Follow Christ once more! Throw off your timidity, renounce your terror; come back into our lives once more! We did not leave you. You left us. We are waiting for you to give the church back to us."

A church I shall always remember is St. Martin-in-the-Fields of London. A paperweight from the original stone is on my desk. It looks so much like our own church. Would God what has been written of her could be written of us:

> The church of the soldiers and the down and outs; the church of the classes and the masses; the church of fellowship and of privacy; the church for the cheerful and the church for the desperate; the church for the healthy and the sick; of the young and of the old. It was the church in which the congregation was no more shocked at hearing the minister pray for the streetwalkers, than pray for school teachers, for the crooks than for the clergy, for blackguards than for bishops. It became a refuge for the unhappy, and a home for the homeless. In short, it was a Christian church.[2]

It is the gospel of which the church is the custodian and propagator which enables us to sit in judgment upon the church. We should at least be grateful that the church is the protector and propagator of the gospel.

Let us not be too harsh in our criticism of those who go to church on Sunday and still live evil lives through the week. Nor should we call them hypocrites. Every man has his good and evil side. The good side which he shows in church on Sunday is not necessarily less real than the evil side which he shows in the market place on Monday. The more fellowship he has with God on Sunday, the more evil will be uprooted from his life. You do not criticize a man for going to a physician because he is not well. Jesus said, "They that be whole need not a physician" (Matt. 9:12).

Paul was always thankful for what is right with the church.

Notes

1. A. S. M. Hutchinson, *One Increasing Purpose* (Boston: Little, Brown & Co., 1925), p. 448.
2. Quoted in Gerald Kennedy (Compiler), *A Second Reader's Notebook* (New York: Harper & Brothers, 1959), p. 60. Used by permission.

6. The Three Greatest Words in the Gospel

Colossians 1:4-5

On wings of deeds the soul must mount!
When we are summoned from afar,
Ourselves, and not our words will count—
Not what we said but what we are![1]

Yet, what we are is often expressed in our words. So much is this so that we are told we shall give an account for every idle word we have spoken (Matt. 12:36).

Words are among the most powerful forces of earth. If you do not believe it, try reading these words of John Charles McNeill without being moved to the foundation of your soul:

Hills wrapped in gray, standing along the West,
Clouds, dimly lighted, gathering slowly;
The star of peace at watch above the crest—
Oh, holy, holy, holy!

We know, O Lord, so little what is best;
Wingless, we move so lowly;
But in thy calm all-knowledge let us rest—
Oh, holy, holy, holy!

Words have power, and the words of the New Testament are powerful because they are empowered by the presence of Christ. They are different from all other words in that they can be interpreted only through him who is the Word of God, who was made flesh to dwell among us. When Paul wrote the immortal hymn to love (1 Cor. 13), he was not simply combining the most sublime words ever assembled. Rather, he was recording his meditations on the character of Christ Jesus. Thus you feel the very presence of Christ as you read the passage.

As we come now to think of the three greatest words in the gospel, remember that they find their meaning in Christ and his redeeming action in earth and in heaven. The greatest words of the gospel are faith, hope, and love. It was Paul who first described the Christian life in terms of these three irreducible elements. Where one of these words is found in the writings of Paul, the others are not faraway.

Every Christian lives in three dimensions of time—the past, present, and future. He lives in the past, for he has a history without which he could not be a man. He lives in the present, for he is a responsible soul obligated to serve God in his own day and generation. He lives in the future, for he is an immortal soul. How can he live concurrently in these three dimensions? He lives in the past by faith, in the present by love, and in the future by hope.[2]

Knowing all this, Paul thanks God for the truth that despite the error in the Colossian congregation still he finds them full of faith, love, and hope. He knows that where these dwell, Christ dwells.

First, we live in the past by faith. By faith we pull the values of the past into the present. It is faith which enables us to reach back and join hands with the apostles and the prophets and, best of all, with the Christ of Galilee. How poor we would be if we could not share in the rich spiritual experiences of those who have gone before us, whom we have not seen, yet by faith most truly believe. By faith we lay hold upon the blessing Jesus promised, "Blessed are they that have not seen, and yet have believed" (John 20:29).

Christian faith is centered in the redeeming action of God in Christ. By his life, death, and resurrection we have been delivered into the kingdom of life eternal.

Yet, not only is Christian faith centered in Christ, it is also sustained by him, for he is the only sphere in which faith can survive. Faith is not the attitude of a man who looks dispassionately upon Christ from a distance and coldly evaluates him. It is the outlook of a man who has surrendered self to Christ and has entered into him who is the actual element in which every Christian lives and moves and has his being.

When by his grace, we are lifted into Christ, faith becomes his gift to us. "For by grace are ye saved through faith; and that not of yourselves: it is the gift of God" (Eph. 2:8).

Furthermore, for Paul, faith was not simply an attitude toward the past; it was the means of pulling the strength of the past into the present. It was the actual working energy which Christ bestows on all who are united with him.

Paul, therefore, in 1 Thessalonians 1:3, could speak of "your work of faith, and labour of love, and patience of hope in our Lord Jesus Christ." Paul thanked God, not for a blind, lethargic acknowledging of the realities of the past on the part of the Colossian Christians, but for the energetic devotion to the living Christ by which the identical blessings Christians had known in the past were known in them. Faith can never be divorced from energetic action.

Dwight L. Moody once said:

I suppose that if all the times I have prayed for faith were put together, it would amount to months. I used to say, "What we want is faith; if we only have faith we can turn Chicago upside down," or rather right side up. I thought that some day faith would come down and strike me like lightning. But faith did not seem to come. One day I read in the tenth chapter of Romans, "Faith cometh by hearing, and hearing by the Word of God." I had closed my Bible and prayed for faith. I now opened my Bible and began to study, and faith has been growing ever since.[3]

Faith includes action: "We walk by faith, not by sight."

The story is told of a man who stretched a strong cable across Niagara Falls, then pushed a wheelbarrow before him as he walked over the cable. A large crowd had gathered to watch him. The people almost held their breath. At last he was safely over, and the crowd cheered and cheered. Then he announced that on the morrow he would push a man over the cable in the wheelbarrow. Many said, "It cannot be done. He can never do it." Nevertheless, a large crowd gathered the next day and waited expectantly to see what would happen. Again it was expressed, "He cannot do it. I know it cannot be done." But a boy was heard to say, "Yes, he can do it; I know he can do it; he has a steady eye." Just then a man stepped up to the boy and said, "Do you really believe it can be done?" The boy answered, "Yes, I am sure he can do it." Then the man said: "I am glad to hear you say that, for I am the man who is going to push the wheelbarrow, and as yet I have not found a man who is willing to ride in it. Come on, let us go."[4]

Faith involves commitment. "Faith, if it hath not works, is dead" (James 2:17). Right believing and compassionate conduct combine to compose Christian character.

Faith is loyal, energetic devotion to Christ, and for this Paul thanked God as he saw it at work in the saints at Colossae. He saw this faith manifested in the love they had toward other Christians. Loyalty to Christ produces love for people. Love is the means by which we live in the present. For if men love not, they are not spiritually alive. We are thus being summoned today by Frank Laubach to love or perish. Long, long ago it was written, "He that loveth not his brother abideth in death" (1 John 3:14).

Henry George once said to Cardinal Manning, "I loved the

people and that brought me to Christ as their best friend and teacher." Cardinal Manning replied, "And I loved Christ and so learned to love the people for whom he died."[5]

> There is . . . a stupendous paradox . . . which is characteristic of all true religion. We must spiritually renounce all other loves for love of God or at least so hold them in subordination to this that we are ready to forego them for its sake; yet when we find God, or rather, when we know ourselves as found of Him, we find in and with him all the loves which for His sake we had foregone.[6]

Richard C. Trench wrote:

> The man is happy, Lord, who love like
> this doth owe:
> Loves thee, his friend in thee, and for
> thy sake, his foe.[7]

Paul was thanking God for that love which forms a Christian brotherhood which transcends ties of kin and race, which forgives and forgets all injuries and animosities and forms a true fellowship of the Spirit.

The third great word of the gospel is hope. Paul thanks God for "the hope which is laid up for you in heaven." This is the means by which the Christian lives in the future. Hope is the anchor of the soul (Heb. 6:19) which is cast in the invisible harbor of a higher shore which assures the vessel of life of a safe arrival in the high country of heaven.

There are those who are offended at the thought of any man's expecting a reward for the good life, who feel that this kind of calculating is foreign to the highest spirit of the gospel. They say, "The good life is its own reward." "Goodness for its own sake," is their motto.

There is much that is noble and praiseworthy in such an ideal. Our Lord would surely say that love of God and of his will is the supreme motivation of the Christian life. Yet, this does not mean that this is the only motive for serving him. Surely it is not the only encouragement for Christian conduct and service. He spoke freely of rewards in heaven. Because man's life has an immortal dimension, it would be irrational for him to refuse to live today so that he would be thankful tomorrow and tomorrow and all the tomorrows because of the rewards of right living.

To be sure, the rewards of eternity must be in terms of the investments. The reward for loving God and serving him is an ever-increasing love for God, a soul ever made more in the image of God and a heart at rest in his presence.

> Hope, like the taper's gleamy light,
>   Adorns the wretch's way;
> And still, as darker glows the night,
>   Emits a brighter ray.
>
> OLIVER GOLDSMITH

Paul speaks of the hope as being laid up in heaven (Col. 1:5). The word *apokeimai,* translated "laid up," was often used in business. It would be found in "storage receipts of grain stored" in a granary, books "housed" in a library, treasures "kept" in a temple. The hope then is here used in the concrete sense of "the object of hope," the "promised blessing," which is represented figuratively as a treasure stored in a heavenly treasure house hidden from the world's view, inestimably precious and forever secure.[8]

Paul thanks God for the character of his readers, but this does not prevent him from thanking God also for their heavenly reward. This is a true part of the gospel. Paul appealed to men in terms of their citizenship in heaven (Phil. 3:20). Peter spoke of the inheritance reserved in heaven (1 Peter 1:4).

The fact that this treasure is laid up means that it lies in the future; it is hidden from human view and is secure forever.

This hope is not solely a flight into the future. It is the inspirer of present faith and love. Paul speaks of faith in Christ and love in the saints because of the hope which is laid up in heaven. The springs of a Christian's conduct are in a higher and better world.

I can never forget those words of Augustine engraved on a stained glass window above the exit of the library in New College at the University of Edinburgh. Emerging from a long day's study, before going out into the murky, old city, I would look up and see those words which served as a constant warning against those who are anchored too much in this world. "All our springs are in thee, dear city of God."

To love one's enemies in this ruthless, competitive society seems to this world the way of the fool. But Paul contended that a man who is to meet the lover of all men in judgment at last is wise only when he loves because he knows that God's way of love will ultimately triumph.

Through hope we cling to the everlasting mercy of God. A missionary in Canada, who had to travel so widely that his visits to the settlements were separated by long intervals of time, visited a settler's home and taught a small, invalid boy the text, "the Lord is my shepherd." He did this by the method of letting each finger represent a word and fitting actions to his words, finally saying, "Remember, always to hold on to the fourth finger—"the Lord is *my* shepherd." When he came back to that home two years later, the boy was not there. He had died in the dark of a winter night and said the mother, "We found him in the morning with his hands outside the coverlet, his left hand clasped round the fourth finger of the right hand."

Christ is our hope and help and he will be our guide even unto death.

Notes

1. William Winter, quoted in Charles L. Wallis (ed.), *A Treasury of Sermon Illustrations* (New York: Abingdon Press, 1950), p. 288. Used by permission.

2. Emil Brunner, *Faith, Hope and Love.* Copyright 1956, W. L. Jenkins (Philadelphia: The Westminster Press; London: Lutterworth Press), p. 13. Used by permission.

3. Quoted in Wallis, *op. cit.,* p. 116. Used by permission.

4. *Ibid.*

5. *Ibid.,* p. 51.

6. William Temple, *Nature, Man and God* (New York: The Macmillan Co., 1956), p. 458.

7. Quoted in Wallis, *op. cit.,* p. 196.

8. Francis W. Beare and G. Preston MacLeod, "The Epistle to the Colossians," *The Interpreter's Bible,* ed. George Buttrick *et al.* (New York: Abingdon Press, 1955), XI, 152.

7. Nature and Work of the Gospel

Colossians 1:6-8

Every true pastor trembles a bit when he stands before a worshiping congregation. He knows that he holds in his hand a book which contains a message which, if received, will rescue men from darkness and deliver them into the kingdom of light and love and life eternal. If it is refused, it may seal their separation from God forever. The gospel is the "savour of death unto death; and . . . the savour of life unto life" (2 Cor. 2:16).

The heart of the Scriptures is the gospel. It is impossible to preach the Bible with understanding without preaching about the gospel. Yet men may stand in pulpits and preach about the gospel all of their days and never preach the gospel.

Knowing this, Paul reminds the Colossian church of "the truth of the gospel; Which is come unto you, as it is in all the world; and bringeth forth fruit, as it doth also in you since the day ye heard of it, and knew the grace of God in truth: As ye also learned of Epaphras our dear fellowservant, who is for you a faithful minister of Christ; Who also declared unto us your love in the Spirit" (Col. 1:5-8).

Here is a concise summary of the nature and work of the gospel.

The gospel is a word. By a word Paul did not mean simply letters on a printed page but a living expression. Paul places the gospel in apposition with the word of truth. The gospel is the word of truth. When Luke, in the prologue of the Gospel, spoke of eyewitnesses of the word (Luke 1:2), he was referring to the living expression of the truth of God in Christ. John's prologue also moves around this living Word.

Here the evangelist tells us how God communicates his saving knowledge and power to man. God is not content to give us ideas about himself and abandon us to our meager powers of intellect to comprehend them. Neither is he content to give us abstract moral principles and laws to govern our conduct. The Christian gospel affirms that he came to earth in his son who is the living word of God incarnate in human flesh. "The Word was made flesh, and dwelt among us, (and we beheld his glory, the glory as of the only begotten of the Father,) full of grace and truth" (John 1:14).

When John wrote his Gospel, there were probably at least a hundred thousand Greeks for every Jew in the church; therefore, he expressed the Christian gospel in terms of words familiar to the Greeks. John had to find a term which would bridge the chasm between the Jewish and the Greek thought patterns. The term he chose was "logos," which we translate "word."

To both Greek and Hebrew minds a word meant far more than spoken syllables. To the Hebrew a word had strange living power. He saw men stirred and stimulated into action by persuasive speech. He saw words do things to people. The word of God had special power. "By the word of the Lord were the heavens made" (Psalm 33:6). Said the psalmist, "He sent his word, and healed them" (Psalm 107:20). The powerful, dynamic, and creative work of God, said the Hebrew, is done by his word.

For the Greek, the idea of the word came first into philosophy about 560 B.C. It emerged first in Ephesus, where John later wrote his Gospel. Heraclitus was the father of the philosophy which held that everything in the universe is constantly changing. In the light of this discovery, he raised the question, if everything is constantly changing, how is it that there is a steady pattern of order which persists throughout this change? His answer was, the logos or the reason of God controls the pattern. Heraclitus thought of the word as the mind of God controlling his creation and every living creature holding the universe in balance and instilling in the mind of man the power to perceive and understand his environment.

John, the evangelist, borrowed this term and filled it with Christian content. He said to Hebrew and Greek alike, "You have been groping for knowledge of the ultimate reality, behind and above this universe, for the creating power that called it into existence, for the intelligence that holds it in balance, for the goodness and grace which floods this grey earth with glory. You will find it in Jesus of Nazareth. All that you need do to see the mind and character and creative power of God is to look at Jesus."

How did John know this? He had seen Jesus do what only God could do. In his presence, hopeless men, out of whose faces all joy and peace had vanished, began to hope again. Weak men, who wanted to do right but had not stamina enough within themselves, who had stumbled and fallen so many times that they had lost self-confidence, found that they could walk uprightly when he walked by their side. Twisted, soiled lives became straight and clean. Timid souls became brave and broken lives healed and restored. No one had ever done what Christ did for men. When John thought of this, he drew the same conclusion as Paul, "God was in Christ, reconciling the world unto himself" (2 Cor. 5:19).

To preach the word is to preach the redeeming, reconciling intervention of God in Christ.

The gospel is the good news, the wondrous glad tidings to be heralded from the housetops. It is the good news that God is the all-loving companion who came down in the man of Nazareth to be the friend and lover of the souls of men. It is the good news that through Christ men may be made right with God, that estranged and alienated souls may be reconciled and gathered to their hearts' true home. The gospel is the old, but ever new, story "that Christ died for our sins according to the scriptures; and that he was buried, and that he rose again the third day according to the scriptures" (1 Cor. 15:3-4).

The gospel, Paul emphasizes, is the final word of truth. The gospel, said Paul, came (and remained with you) as the final disclosure of God. It is not the wild speculation of the overheated imagination of an armchair philosopher nor the theory of a secluded mystic but concrete, historic fact. No science of any age can sit in judgment upon this truth, for this is the truth by which all science and all secular knowledge must be judged. Few things would be more exasperating to the great apostle than to hear the modern dilettante of the pulpit quote some scientist who has acknowledged the truth of the Christian gospel as though such tribute were another feather in the cap of the gospel.

William Barclay writes: "All previous religions could be entitled 'guesses about God.' The Christian gospel gives a man, not guesses, but certainties about God."[1] Rousseau once wrote, "The Gospels bear such an imprint of truth, they are so striking, so utterly inimitable, that were one to consider them as having been invented, the inventor would be greater than He with whom they deal."[2]

Richard Ellsworth Day has called D. L. Moody the "accolade of fire." I heard Dr. Day tell in a lecture of how Moody, who began his ministry during a great spiritual drought, always insisted that the day of our Lord's power would come again. Much of Moody's physical power was inherited from his mother. When she was eighty years of age, she wrote him a letter saying, "I still do all my work except combing my hair. When I get too weary, I just get down on my knees and let the Lord caress me."

Dr. Day received the Bible of Moody's mother and read the passages which were marked with her tears. One day her husband came home ill and was dead in two hours. He left her with seven children and two under her heart yet to be born. No wonder her soul found comfort in Jeremiah 49:11: "Leave thy fatherless children, I will preserve them alive; and let thy widows trust in me."

Moody's stalwart virility was from his mother. He was the sort of man who could switch out the light and get into bed before the room got dark. When the Civil War roared down on America, seven times he went down to the front to preach to the soldiers.

Then came Moody's time of spiritual dearth when "that small black spot of working too much without waiting for the voice of God began to get him." Two women had said to him at the close of a service, "At no place is the unsurrendered will of man more dangerous than when it is serving altars."

Moody was trying to preach in Chicago. "It was one of those days," said Dr. Day, "when it was so hot if a dog should chase a cat, they would both walk." Moody had told many stories, yet with no power. He went on to New York and preached; still there was no power. At the close of the service an old woman came forward and said, "Mr. Moody, if you would just tell us something about the Bible it would be a great blessing to us." He went back to Chicago and centered his preaching in the Bible. At the close of the first service, his former critics came forward and said, "Now lad, walk softly. Jehovah hath dealt with thee!"

Paul sees the universality of the gospel as a testimony to its truth. The fact that it bears fruit everywhere is a proof of its validity. He does not mean that its widespread popularity establishes its truth, for error is often more popular than truth. There has never been a time when the majority of humanity endorsed the Christian faith. Yet Paul does insist that truth is by nature universal. The local heresy at work in the church is not recognized elsewhere as truth. Therefore, it is to be refused.

The truth of the gospel is for all men. Therefore, our Lord gave his solemn command, "Go ye into all the world" (Mark 16:15). He was emphasizing our responsibility to proclaim the gospel extensively—embracing the geography of the world—but also intensively. Go ye into the world of law and preach the gospel—into the world of medicine, the world of education, the world of business, the world of politics, the world of entertainment, the world of physics. Into all worlds within this world the herald of the cross must go.

Francis W. Beare sees Paul's statement that the gospel is bearing fruit in all the world not so much as a pardonable exaggeration of an enthusiast as an assertion of the uniformity of the gospel. Wherever it is preached it is the same gospel.[3]

E. F. Scott calls this statement of Paul, "a wild exaggeration, for the Church as yet consisted of tiny handfuls of people, almost unnoticed in the great empire which itself was only a fraction of the world."[4]

But Paul sees in these words the promise of a worldwide community. To this G. Preston MacLeod replies, "Though rudimentary and weak, centers of Christian teaching and influence were already established in every major quarter of Roman civilization."[5] L. B. Radford points out that the gospel had already been proclaimed in most provinces of the Empire. He mentions Palestine, Syria, Cilicia, Galatia, Phrygia, Asia, Pontus, Bithynia, Macedonia, Achaia, Italy, with strong probability also of Egypt, Africa, and perhaps Gaul.[6]

In addition to the actual geographical conquest, Paul is here giving expression to the daring of faith, just as the psalmist did when he wrote, "Glorious things are spoken of thee" (Psalm 87:3). Jerusalem was then nothing but a desert. He was speaking of the glorious city that was to be. This was the daring of faith, for at the time Jerusalem lay in utter desolation. A. F. Kirkpatrick has written:

It seems best then to suppose that the Psalm was written (like Psalm LXXXV) after the Return from Babylon, to cheer the drooping spirits of those returned exiles who were in danger of being utterly disheartened by the disappointing contrast between the weakness and insignificance of their little community, and the grandeur and magnificence of the prophetic promises of the future glory and greatness of Zion.[7]

The universality of the gospel means that it is for every man. William Barclay reminds us:

There are very few things in this world which are open to all men. A man's mental calibre decides the studies which he can undertake. A man's social class decides the circles amidst which he will move. A man's material wealth determines the material possessions which he can amass. A man's particular gifts and talents decide the things which he can do. But the message of the gospel, and the joy and the peace of the gospel, are open without exception to all men.[8]

Paul is here refuting the heresy at work in Colossae, contending that it is a local perversion of truth, while the gospel has passed the supreme test. First, it has been demonstrated as true on a universal scale. Second, it has passed the pragmatic test. It has been effectual in the production of fruit wherever it has been proclaimed. Third, it has the power to grow and increase.

Wherever the gospel is proclaimed, individual character is changed and with it the character of the community. Sinners are transformed into saints. Crime-ridden communities are made into respectable places. Cruelty gives way to compassion. Selfishness is replaced with charity. Strife gives way to peace.

At the center of the gospel is God's grace. It is not a message of the heavy demands which a tyrannical power above would impose upon us—some oppressive burden to be carried or some daunting duty which must be performed. The gospel is not a detailed account of impossible demands. It is a wondrous story of what God offers to give to all who will receive.

Finally, Paul emphasizes that this gospel is made known to men by men. God's gift flows through human channels. All who receive it are obligated to pass it on. This is the strange paradox of the gospel—the divine word must be spoken by men.

Those at Colossae had received the gospel through Epaphras, their pastor. He was a true shepherd of souls who brought the problem of his people to the apostle. Yet, they had turned against the very man who had led them to Christ. These heretics had no doubt contended that he was far too simple to be the pastor of the intellectuals and far too naïve to have any influence on such a cosmopolitan city. Despite their criticism, Epaphras did not retaliate. He did not say to Paul, "This is a congregation of heretics and reprobates." Rather, said Paul, he "declared unto us your love in the Spirit" (Col. 1:8). Everything that Paul commended in them had been told him by Epaphras.

Then Paul encourages them to put down their criticism of their pastor, declaring, "Epaphras our dear fellowservant, who is for you a faithful minister of Christ" (Col. 1:7). No one is smaller than when he thinks the only way he can make himself big is by criticizing his pastor.

Notes

1. William Barclay, *The Letters to the Philippians, Colossians and Thessalonians* (2d ed.; Philadelphia: The Westminster Press, 1959), p. 128. By permission The Westminster Press and The Saint Andrew Press.
2. Quoted in Kennedy, *op. cit.,* p. 156.
3. Beare and MacLeod, *op. cit.,* p. 153.
4. Scott, *op. cit.,* p. 16.
5. Beare and MacLeod, *loc. cit.*
6. L. B. Radford, *"The Epistle to the Colossians and the Epistle to Philemon," The Westminster Commentaries,* ed. Walter Lock and D. C. Simpson (London: Methuen & Co., 1931), pp. 151-52.
7. A. F. Kirkpatrick, *The Book of Psalms* (Cambridge: Cambridge University Press, 1939), p. 519. Used by permission.
8. Barclay, *op. cit.*

8. Three Great Gifts from God

Colossians 1:9-11

Every Christian should give reverent attention when he reads the prayer of an apostle. For here we have a rich insight into the deepest things of the spiritual life. The thanksgiving of the great apostle is followed by certain concrete petitions. He writes,

> And so, from the day we heard of it [their love in the spirit], we have not ceased to pray for you, asking that you may be filled with the knowledge of his will in all spiritual wisdom and understanding, to lead a life worthy of the Lord, fully pleasing to him, bearing fruit in every good work and increasing in the knowledge of God. May you be strengthened with all power, according to his glorious might, for all endurance and patience with joy (Col. 1:9-11, RSV).

This simple, yet comprehensive prayer, pleads for four things—the highest knowledge, the knowledge of the will of God; the deepest understanding, which is the ability to discern between the false and the true; power to live a worthy and fruitful life; and finally, for the bestowal of three great gifts: spiritual endurance, patience, and joy.

Prayer's foremost purpose is the discovery of the will of God. Prayer is not so much trying to persuade God to hear our voice as it is an attempt to hear the voice of God. A pagan prays to persuade God to do the will of man. A Christian prays that he might discover and do the will of God. Dr. William Barclay has written, "It so often happens that in prayer we are really saying, 'Thy will be changed,' when we ought to be saying, 'Thy will be done.' The first object of prayer is not so much to speak to God, as it is to listen to God."[1]

The Gnostics were interested in a knowledge that would lift them above their fellow men. "The Christian," said Paul, "is not interested in knowledge for knowledge's sake but for the sake of doing the will of God." He prays, "May you increase in every good work through the knowledge of God." The knowledge of God is simultaneously a revelation of the will of God. God is not concerned with satisfying our speculative curiosity but with building his kingdom through making known his will. The Gnostics would know God without being constrained to obey him. Not so for a Christian, for to him every disclosure of God is a command.

Paul constantly warned his followers against false wisdom which he calls the wisdom of the present age (1 Cor. 2:6). "Where is the wise man? Where is the scribe? Where is the debater of this age? Has not God made foolish the wisdom of the world?" (1 Cor. 1:20, RSV). "For our boast is this, the testimony of our conscience that we have behaved in the world, and still more toward you, with holiness and godly sincerity, not by earthly wisdom but by the grace of God" (2 Cor. 1:12, RSV).

The knowledge *(epignōsin)* for which Paul prayed is a knowledge which penetrates and grasps the will of God. The spiritual wisdom for which he intercedes is the special ability to discern between the true and the false which is not made possible through superior intelligence but through the guidance of the Holy Spirit. It is spiritual wisdom in the sense that it is the result of loyal service to Christ rather than the exercise of superior intelligence.

This highest wisdom binds a Christian to ever declare that the most rational fact that this mad earth has ever seen is Jesus.

True spiritual wisdom and understanding leads men into walking worthily of the Lord, a life fashioned after the life of our Lord so that the outside world would be reminded of Jesus. The lost world would ask, what makes this life so different? Whose image and superscription is in this life? And others would answer, it is the image and superscription of Jesus.

In refuting the Greek intellectualism Paul always placed the emphasis upon the will as the avenue over which true knowledge travels into human personality. He could say with John, "If any man will to do his will, he shall know of the doctrine" (John 7:17).

The knowledge which does not bear fruit in every good work is not the knowledge of God. Furthermore, it is the nature of the knowledge of God to be constantly increasing. The more of God we know, the more we want to know; and the more we open our hearts to fuller revelations, the more we follow him, the more guidance and knowledge he gives us.

"The wisdom [*sophia*] that is from above is first pure, then peaceable . . . full of mercy and good fruits, without partiality, and without hypocrisy" (James 3:17). This is the wisdom which comes through the experience of doing the will of God, not through speculation.

To accomplish the fulfilment of God's will requires tremendous power. Paul, therefore, prayed that believers may be strengthened with all power. He saw the need of a terrific force to turn a bad man into a good man, for all the sin in this world and all the evil powers of darkness are aligned against God. Yet, God's full power is pledged to the Christian. In the New Testament, glory is the light in which God dwells. It is God's manifested nature. Here Paul sees God's nature manifested as power.

This power of God is pledged to give every Christian three great gifts:

First, "fortitude" or "endurance": *Hupomonē* is the ability to withstand every evil assault on the soul and to do so in such a manner as to translate it into glory. When disease, failure, loss of friends, and all manner of adversity befall you, *hupomonē* is the ability to handle life and to come through in shining triumph. Only divine power can provide this kind of fortitude.

Arrius, a Roman, spoke to Ben-Hur, in Lew Wallace's novel:

"The hortator tells me thou art his best rower."
"The hortator is very kind," the rower answered.
"Hast thou seen much service?"
"About three years."
"At the oars?"
"I cannot recall a day of rest from them."
"The labor is hard; few men bear it a year without breaking, and thou—thou art but a boy."
"The noble Arrius forgets that the spirit hath much to do with endurance. By its help the weak sometimes thrive, when the strong perish."

The second great gift God's power provides is patience. *Makrothumia* is that long-suffering spirit which enables a Christian to deal with malicious men who make life unpleasant and often bitter. It holds him above despair when ruthless foes would beat him down. Dr. Barclay said, "*Makrothumia* is the spirit which never loses patience with, belief in, and hope for men."[2]

This inward power which every Christian recognizes as not his own gives a spirit of joy.

The spirit of fortitude *(hupomonē)*, which causes a man to refuse to be a coward in the face of danger and to refuse to give way to despondency when misfortune falls, and the spirit of patience *(makrothumia)*, which causes a man to refuse to retaliate in wrath against his enemies, often have a hardening effect upon the soul, which leaves the heart hard and cold and wrapped in gloom. Then it is that Christ's power shines through to bring joy. Christian joy is the "laughter which floats on tears." Joy which has not been refined in the fires of suffering is much too superficial and shallow to sustain us in the dark night of the soul.

There is an old German legend which tells of the man who built his castle on the Rhine:

From crag to crag and from turret to turret he hung wires, hoping that the winds as they blew upon this great Aeolian harp, might make sweet music. Long and patiently he waited, and round his castle winds from the four corners of heaven blew; and still no music came. But one night there arose a hurricane tossing the Rhine to fury; the black sky was stabbed with lightning and the thunder rolled, the earth trembled, and the winds were mad and shrieking. The baron went to his great castle door to view the terrifying scene—when hark! the sound of music like angels singing through the storm. And suddenly, he realized what had happened. His harp, strung from crag to crag, had come to life at last. The tempest had given it a soul.

That oft-told tale goes down to the heart of life's deep mystery. How often it is only when trouble comes that a man's true quality stands revealed.[3]

God bestows upon the faithful three great spiritual gifts: spiritual endurance in every hard circumstance; patience with every obnoxious person; and in the midst of it all, joy which the world cannot give and cannot take away.

Notes

1. Barclay, *op. cit.*, p. 130.
2. *Ibid.*, p. 132.
3. James S. Stewart, *The Gates of New Life* (New York: Charles Scribner's Sons, 1940), pp. 34-35. By permission Charles Scribner's Sons and T. & T. Clark.

9. Life's Highest Inheritance

Colossians 1:12-14

Few things in life are more enthralling than the thought of receiving a great inheritance. A television program, "The Millionaire," centers around the utterly unsuspecting person who is suddenly handed a cashier's check for a million dollars. Have you ever allowed your imagination to engage in flights of fancy, thinking of what you would do if such good fortune should befall you?

When Paul speaks of an inheritance in which Christians are to share, he expects our hearts to beat faster in quickened elation and strong anticipation. He reminds the Colossian Christians that they have been qualified to receive a great inheritance. It is the inheritance which God would now bestow upon every man. Once it was reserved for the chosen people of God—Israel. Now it is open to the Gentiles whom God has "qualified" to share the inheritance of the saints in light.

The verb *hikanoō* translated "qualify," comes from the adjective *hikanos,* meaning suitable, capable, competent. It means, therefore, that God has made men capable of sharing the lot of the saints. It is God who qualifies men. Too often this is interpreted to mean that since God does it, there is no real change in men. A. S. Peake contends that the passage refers to the status of man and not to his character.[1] Yet vital Christianity cannot spring from such forensic concepts which contend that God gives us an inheritance without making us capable of receiving it. Paul insists that God has qualified us.

Klēros, the word translated inheritance, means "lot" and goes back to those stirring times when the Promised Land was apportioned by lot to the tribes of Israel (Josh. 13:6). Paul takes this historic incident and tells us that just as God assigned an earthly territory to his people, even so, through Christ, he now assigns to them a place in the presence of God forever.

Klēros also designated the lot assigned to veteran soldiers as their abiding place after the days of their warfare had ended. All of this speaks of the hope which is laid up in heaven (Col. 1:5) for the servants of Christ when they lay down the weapons of their warfare and they are received into their final rest.

"Saints in light" (Col. 1:12) refers to our share in the lot of the life of the saints. In the Old Testament, light is the metaphor of salvation. "The Lord is my light and my salvation" (Psalm 27:1). So Paul used it to mean the world of light where God dwells and has destined his own to be.

Before Agrippa, Paul declared his work to be "to open their eyes, and to turn them from darkness to light, and from the power of Satan unto God, that they may receive forgiveness of sins, and inheritance among them which are sanctified by faith that is in me" (Acts 26:18).

God has qualified them to share the inheritance of the saints in light by delivering them from the dominion of darkness, by re-establishing them in the kingdom of his beloved Son, and by redeeming them and forgiving their sins. Here we are given the three essentials for sharing the inheritance of the saints: We must be rescued, re-established, and redeemed.

First, there must be a rescue. Paul never thinks of entrance into the Christian life as a casual acceptance of certain bland religious doctrines. He uses a strong and stirring word. You have been rescued! The heavenly warrior with blood-red banners, mounted on the white horse of a conqueror, followed by the armies of heaven, has come to your rescue. He has come to tread the winepress of the fierceness of the wrath of God Almighty (Rev. 19:13-15). "Who is this that cometh from Edom, with dyed garments from Bozrah? this that is glorious in his apparel, travelling in the greatness of his strength? I that speak in righteousness, mighty to save" (Isa. 63:1).

The word for rescue implies the perilous and wretched condition of men outside of Christ. The dark dungeons of depravity have imprisoned them and the chains which bound them were the chains of sin. The minions of darkness hold them.

For all of its magnificent beauty, one of the most distressing sights of earth is the Bridge of Sighs in Venice. Spanning one of the romantic canals, it connects a hall of justice with a prison. When men were condemned, they were led across the Bridge of Sighs to be imprisoned in narrow stone cells for the remainder of their days—cells where the rays of the sun never enter, where joy comes no more and hope dies. To be rescued by Christ is like being released from such a prison house of doom and despair.

The word "rescue" also implies the struggle in which Christ engaged with the minions of darkness of Calvary. This rescue was exceedingly costly for God.

Into the shadows of disbelief, doubt, and death, into the darkness of delusion, defeat, and despair, Christ breaks like a blazing light. Thus it was that Bilney the martyr, upon reading for the first time that Christ came into the world to save sinners, declared that it was like the dawn breaking on a dark night.

"The rescue of a Christian," said Paul, "takes place at a specific, decisive moment." The aorist tense of the verb points to an act in an exact moment. That moment is the time of conversion. Conversion is the transition of the soul from sin into grace and is the most important transition the immortal soul of man ever makes. Even more important is the transition of the soul from sin to grace than is the transition at death from grace to glory.

When by the grace of God man is lifted out of the darkness of sin into the light, he begins then to breathe the air of God's higher kingdom. When death comes, a Christian simply moves from one province to another of the same country. The transition from the state of sin to the state of grace is a greater change than the transition out of this world to the world to come; for it is like coming out of gross darkness into marvelous light, while moving from grace to glory is moving from light to fuller light. We have been rescued from the dominions of darkness and made to dwell in the light of his glory and grace.

The gnostic philosophers who were perverting the faith of the Colossians believed that angelic beings who had fallen from heaven had produced this world and were, therefore, in control of it. These angels were identified with the spirits enthroned in the planets. Paul called them the potentates of the dark present (Eph. 6:12), the world rulers of this darkness.

By his atoning death, Paul sees Christ as triumphing over these powers, and through his atonement he rescued men from their tyranny. The false teachers in the Colossian church contended that either men must conciliate these powers or ally themselves with superior powers which would protect them.

Paul contends that since Christ conquered all the powers which converged on Calvary to crucify him, by rising from the dead, he is, therefore, above all other powers. In him we are fully liberated from all malign forces which would enslave and crush us. In him God has rescued us from the region where darkness holds dominion. The subjective genitive means the dominion which darkness exercises. For Paul darkness was not simply a state but a power which exercises authority. The supramundane power of God came down into our darkness to rescue us.

In loving-kindness Jesus came
My soul in mercy to reclaim,
And from the depths of sin and shame
Thro' grace He lifted me.
From sinking sand He lifted me,
With tender hand He lifted me,
From shades of night to plains of light,
O praise His name, He lifted me!

CHARLES H. GABRIEL

In the second place, Paul tells us that Christ has qualified us for the inheritance of the saints in light by re-establishing us in the kingdom of his beloved Son.

Methistēmi, to translate or transplant or re-establish, is a colorful word borrowed from the mass deportations of the ancient world. When one nation conquered another, the total population of the conquered people was transplanted to another land. This was true when the Northern Kingdom was carried into Assyria and when the populace of Jerusalem and the Southern Kingdom were carried into Babylon.

The Jews in Colossae had been deported in the time of Antiochus. They knew what Paul meant when he used this term. It said to them that God in Christ had transplanted them completely from one kingdom to another, from the sphere of depravity and darkness into the kingdom of the Son of his love.

This kingdom is the expression of his love. This term calls to mind the voice from heaven at the baptism of the Saviour. "This is my beloved Son, in whom I am well pleased" (Matt. 3:17). He came to identify himself with the race he came to redeem. If you would see God's love in its fulness, look at the Son of his love and never forget that his kingdom is the kingdom of love.

Finally, Christ qualifies us for the inheritance of the saints in light by redeeming us. "It is by His Son alone that we have been redeemed and have had our sins forgiven" (Col. 1:13-14).[2]

To redeem meant the act of loosing a slave from his bonds. The real background for *lutrōsis* is in Numbers 35:31: "Accept no ransom for the life of a murderer" (RSV). Jesus said, "For the Son of man also came not to be served but to serve, and to give his life as a ransom *(lutron)* for many" (Mark 10:45, RSV).

In Mark 8:37, Jesus said, "What shall a man give in exchange for his soul?" Once the soul is lost you cannot buy it back. He probably had in mind Psalm 49:7, "None of them can by any means redeem his brother, nor give to God a ransom for him."

Man cannot ransom or redeem himself. Therefore, Christ came to ransom us, to redeem us from bondage, from the slavery to self, to sin, and to fear.

Redemption for Paul meant primarily a mighty act of divine power, such as the deliverance from Egypt in the days of Moses or the deliverance from the Assyrian or Babylonian captivity.

To refute the idea that men needed more than Christ to assure them of complete redemption, Paul combines these strongest of terms, saying, "Christ has rescued, re-established, and redeemed us to show that we need no further propitiation of any kind of higher powers." Christ has rescued us from the dominion of darkness, transplanted us into a kingdom over which the powers of darkness have no dominion, redeemed and reconciled us.

This total deliverance has its summation in the forgiveness of sins. Forgiveness shatters the shackles which enslave the soul. For Paul forgiveness meant moral deliverance made possible through the reconciling power of love.

"Salvation," said Paul to the Colossian Christians, "is not attained, as the false teachers are insisting, by intellectual speculation, by making a religion of our own or by causing the truth once for all delivered to the saints to conform to the culture of our age, nor through the mastery of mystic formulas, nor ceremonial rites, nor through the discovery of some secret password embedded in esoteric theosophy. Salvation is rather the gift of God who by

Christ Jesus has broken the power of sin by a forgiveness which reconciles man to God and gives him God's attitude toward sin.

"In whom" we have redemption. This means we must enter into him. Just as Jesus identified himself utterly with humanity, so must we identify ourselves utterly with him. The summation of redemption is that in Christ we have cleansing, forgiveness, and a fresh start.

Notes

1. Peake, *op. cit.*, p. 500.
2. From *The New Testament in Modern English,* © J. B. Phillips, 1958. This and subsequent quotations from the Phillips translation used with permission of The Macmillan Co.

10. The Reconciling Saviour

Colossians 1:15-18

No loftier description of the Saviour appears in the writings of Paul than we have in this passage. It is the most impressive passage and the most comprehensive Christology set down in this epistle. It is remarkably similar to the prologue of John's Gospel.

So sublime is it in its thought, so beautifully balanced in its meter, so mellifluous in its language, that it might well have been one of the early Christian hymns. The "kenosis" passage in Philippians 2:5-11 is almost certainly an early Christian hymn, bearing evidence that liturgical worship came very early into the Christian church.

This surpassingly sublime passage speaks first of Christ's relation to God, then of his relation to the universe, and finally of his relation to the church.

Look first at the godward aspect. He is the image of the invisible God. The great question for ancient man was how the unseen, eternal God can communicate with mere creatures. The gnostic answer was through emanations from the high, good God which gravitate lower and lower until one is low enough and far enough removed from God to touch the defiling earth without defiling God. Paul said, "Not so, if the high God of heaven is made known, he must come down in his very image as a mediator who is not an intermediate being but one who is fully identified with God and fully identified with man."

Christ Jesus is the image of God, the bearer of the divine might and majesty. Ancient Egyptians worshiped the Pharaohs, whom they identified with Horus, the son of (the unseen) Osiris. "Tutankhamen" means "living image of Amen." The idea of a man's being the living image of God was not new in the first century.

In 1 Corinthians 11:7, Paul calls man the image and glory of God. Furthermore, he claims that "just as we have borne the image of the man of dust, we shall also bear the image of the man of heaven" (1 Cor. 15:49, RSV). "And we all, with unveiled face, beholding the glory of the Lord, are being changed into his likeness [image] from one degree of glory to another; for this comes from the Lord who is the Spirit" (2 Cor. 3:18, RSV).

Now, the whole gospel is bound up in the fact that Christ was not a newcomer at Bethlehem. He was in the beginning with God (John 1:1). The term "first-born" is a messianic idea. The writer of the Hebrews so uses it when he speaks of "when he brings the first-born into the world" (Heb. 1:6, RSV).

Paul carries the concept of Christ higher than does the author of Hebrews, who calls him the image of God (Heb. 1:2-14). Paul calls him the first-born of all creation (Col. 1:15, RSV). He does not belong to the order of all creation. He is *prōtotokos,* prior to it in point of time and superior to it in point of dignity. The thought goes back to Psalm 89:27: "I will make him my firstborn, higher than the kings of the earth." The first-born is the heir and destined ruler. Israel was called God's first-born among the nations. "And thou shalt say unto Pharaoh, Thus saith the Lord, Israel is my son, even my firstborn" (Ex. 4:22).

Paul was refuting the pernicious gnostic dualism which was contending that the world was not God's world, that the world is essentially evil. All things material therein are evil. In essence they were saying, "Christ could not, therefore, have had a real body." Paul answers in Colossians 2:9, that the fulness of the Godhead dwells in him *(sōmatikōs)* in bodily form. To the Gnostics, Jesus was a spirit who only appeared to have a body. Therefore, said they, "when he walked, he left no footprints." To refute this, Paul speaks of the body of his flesh (Col. 1:22).

To the Greeks the word *eikōn,* which we translate "image," also meant a portrait. William Barclay calls attention to a papyrus letter from a soldier, called Apion, to his father, Epimachus. At the close he wrote, "I send you a little portrait *(eikonion)* [diminutive form of *eikōn*] of myself printed by Euctemon."[1] In Jesus we see the portrait of the invisible God.

Paul uses a genitive of comparison which means first-born before all creation. The most furious controversy ever fought in Christendom was at the Council of Nicea (A.D. 325) between Athanasius and Arius over whether or not Christ was to be considered as a part of creation or as being unique and above creation. It was ruled that Jesus was the first begotten, not the first created. Begotten of God means that he was made exactly like him. Origen held the theory of the eternal generation of the Son. Said he, "The generation of the Son took place in eternity where the time sequence has no significance."

Look, then, at Christ's relation to the universe. "For in him all things were created, in heaven and on earth, visible and invisible, whether thrones or dominions or principalities or authorities—all things were created through him and for him" (Col. 1:16, RSV).

The false teachers of Colossae believed that the heavenly bodies possessed souls and that they stood in closest relation to the spirit world. Said they, "These are the spirits with which men need to ally themselves to assure their safe passage to the high dwelling place of God."

Paul answers that Christ is the creator of all things in heaven and on earth—visible and invisible—all things material and spiritual and to make it even more explicit, he even lists the highest of angelic rulers as the creation of Christ.

The angelic hierarchy was fully developed in first-century Judaism. The Book of Enoch overflows with it. In the seventh heaven, Enoch described "a very great light and all the fiery hosts of great archangels, and incorporeal powers and lordships and principalities and powers; cherubim and seraphim, thrones and the watchfulness of many eyes" (The Slavonic Enoch, XX,I).

Paul is simply insisting that of the totality of powers there is not one which Christ has not created. They are all, therefore, subordinate to him. They were created by him and for him in that they must ultimately serve his purpose. He will never serve theirs.

Not only is Christ before all things but in him all things *(sunestēken)* hold together. The perfect tense denotes a state or condition in the universe as an ordered system.

Not only is Christ at the beginning of creation and at the end he is also in between as the divine sustainer. The world is full of centripetal forces. Without Christ this universe would pull apart and disintegrate. In effect, Paul was saying to the Christians in Colossae, "If you have to conciliate all these powers, you have no security at all, but if Christ is the vanguard and the center and at the end, how serene then can be your rest in Christ."

As Christ is the principle of unity in the universe, the Christian must be completely united in his devotion to him. Paul, therefore, said, "This one thing I do." His life was totally integrated and united in Christ.

We are all moving, not toward extinction, but toward Christ. When the shouting and the tumult of life die, the last word is Christ. What is the goal toward which creation moves? What is the end of all things? Paul answers, "We shall all stand before the judgment seat of God" (Rom. 14:10, RSV).

We shall all be measured by the stature of Christ. Life is only livable on Christ's plan. For at the end of the road every man must meet Christ. Beyond western civilization, beyond this age and all ages, beyond this world and all worlds, stands the shepherd with his staff and his rod.

Finally, Paul contends that the same power that holds this universe together holds the church together. "He is the head of the body, the church" (Col. 1:18). This means that the church is no isolated, wayside shrine. It belongs at the center of a Christian culture. It is a part of the plan of all creation. Creation finds its meaning and mission in the message which Christ has committed to his church, for creation was made for redemption.

The church is the living body of Christ which goes on doing the work of Christ, bearing the griefs, carrying the sorrows of humanity, and leading men to God. This metaphor of the body is very similar to that of the vine. "I am the true vine. . . . As the branch cannot bear fruit by itself, unless it abides in the vine, neither can you, unless you abide in me" (John 15:1-4, RSV).

In the church Christ and men are made one flesh. Paul describes the family duties in terms of Christ's relationship to the church. "Even so husbands should love their wives as their own bodies. He who loves his wife loves himself. For no man ever hates his own flesh, but nourishes and cherishes it, as Christ does the church, because we are members of his body" (Eph. 5:28-30, RSV). Christ is the head of the church in the sense that the head of the body directs its activities and causes the body to serve the head.

He is the beginning, the source from which the church comes and the first-born from the dead. The dead could not be the head of the church. He is not a dead founder but a living presence. By his resurrection he became the immortal conqueror. "Christ being raised from the dead will never die again; death no longer has dominion over him" (Rom. 6:9, RSV).

This makes him supreme in all things. These magnificent descriptions of the Son of man cause us to sing with fervent souls:

Jesus, my Shepherd, Brother, Friend,
  My Prophet, Priest, and King,
My Lord, my Life, my Way, my End,
  Accept the praise I bring.

JOHN NEWTON

Notes

1. Barclay, *op. cit.*, p. 142.

11. The Fulness of God

Colossians 1:19-20

The ancient world was full of many gods. Writing of idols and idol worship, Paul said, "We know that an idol is nothing in the world, and that there is none other God but one. For though there be that are called gods, whether in heaven or in earth, (as there be gods many, and lords many,) but to us there is but one God, the Father, of whom are all things, and we in him; and one Lord Jesus Christ, by whom are all things, and we by him" (1 Cor. 8:4-6).

In the days of Josiah there was great idolatory in the land. There were vessels in the temple of the Lord, made for Baal and for all the host of heaven (2 Kings 23:4). Josiah ordered them burned. He purified the temple of its abominations, and of him it was written: "And like unto him was there no king before him, that turned to the Lord with all his heart, and with all his soul, and with all his might, according to all the law of Moses; neither after him arose there any like him" (v. 25). He insisted that the unity of God demanded the unity of man's worship and service to him.

In Colossae there were those who had endorsed Christ as belonging to the grand family of many gods. They could not be honest and refuse him this dignity and honor. Yet, like Mahatma

Gandhi, they concluded "I could not assign to Jesus of Nazareth a solitary throne above the universe, for there have been many incarnations of God." They were willing, like the modern Hindu, to place him alongside Gautama the Buddha, and Moses, and all others with unique religious genius. But Paul insisted that the gospel inhered not in the appearance upon earth of another religious genius but in the total disclosure of the totality of God. He is to have the pre-eminence in all things.

The skeptics declared, "There must be some weakness in him, for did not the powers of darkness put him to death?"

Paul answered, "Yes, the evil powers of earth can kill but they cannot conquer death. Christ went down before them to prove that he is above them."

Since Christ is the first-born of the dead, he is exalted above all powers. In this he is utterly unique and above all spiritual powers. Furthermore, his very death in the hands of God was made the channel of reconciliation for all men and all things in God.

J. B. Phillips translates our passage: "It was in Him that the full nature of God chose to live, and through Him God planned to reconcile in His own Person, as it were, everything on earth and everything in heaven by virtue of the sacrifice of the Cross" (Col. 1:19-20).

Still, today are there those who wish a mild, malleable, ameliorating principle for a religion rather than the worship and service of a highly exalted, supreme Lord. Many still insist on accommodating Christianity to their own whims. For many Christianity seems to be a tale at least twice removed from the only authentic source, the holy Scriptures. This is the primary reason many of us can be very religious and at the same time very unchristian.

In his novel *The Wonderful Year,* William J. Locke tells us how the image of Christ becomes so blurred. One of the characters explains the odd phenomenon of a French woman who was very religious and at the same time very unchristian. Wrote he:

The Bible taught the Church the beautiful history of Jesus Christ. The Church told a Bishop. The Bishop told a priest. The priest told the wife of a sub-prefect. The wife of the sub-prefect told the wife of the mayor. The wife of the mayor told the elderly, unmarried sister of the corn-chandler, and the unmarried sister of the corn-chandler told Clothilde. And that's all she [Clothilde] knows about Christianity.[1]

When Paul wrote "For in him all the fulness of God was pleased to dwell" (Col. 1:19, RSV), the word which he used for fulness (pleroma) was a technical term which all his readers would readily recognize. It meant the sum total. It is so used in the Septuagint where Psalm 24:1 reads, "The earth is the Lord's, and the *fulness* thereof." In classical Greek the word was sometimes used of a ship's crew. The "pleroma" was the full complement of the ship, the full crew.

In the incipient gnosticism of first-century Colossae "pleroma" meant the totality of the innumerable emanations from God. The Colossian heretics had contended that Christ was but one member in the "pleroma" or the totality of God, one among the multitude of emanations. Paul emphatically refused the idea that the powers of the deity are distributed among a host of mediating spirits. He rather insisted, as Lightfoot puts it, "The aggregate of the divine attributes, virtues, energies" resides in Christ alone.

These dwell in Christ to make possible the salvation of mankind. For when God is represented in the Scriptures as dwelling, it is always for the specific purpose of bringing personal salvation.

If you would see the fulness of God's attributes, look at Christ. His power causes the angry waves of the sea to subside, but even more it stills the storm in the souls of men. If you would see God's wisdom, you will find it in its fulness, not in Solomon, but in Christ who spake as never man spake. If you would see God's consuming pity and compassion, you must see it, not in Jeremiah, the weeping prophet, but in Jesus who wept over Jerusalem.

If you would see God's forgiving mercy, you will find it in its fulness, not in Moses who cried, "Now, if thou wilt forgive their sin—; and if not, blot me, I pray thee, out of thy book which thou hast written" (Ex. 32:32), but in Christ who when he was reviled, reviled not again. Upon his wondrous cross Christ stopped dying long enough that through his anguish might shine a spirit which could never be crucified as he prayed "Father, forgive them; for they know not what they do" (Luke 23:34).

"This is what God is like," said Paul. And if this cannot reconcile all men to God and to one another and bring harmony and balance to this earthly order, there is no power in the heavens, on the earth, or under the earth, in time or in eternity that can.

Notes

1. William J. Locke, *The Wonderful Year* (New York: John Lane Co., 1917), pp. 239-40.

12. Peace Through His Cross

Colossians 1:20-23

Mankind now possesses military power of which the apostles never dreamed. Yet the truth taught by the apostles remains. This kind of power which we now possess in such abundance is ineffectual in bringing peace. We are primarily concerned today with the adequacy of our defense.

We were reminded recently of the fact that our nation, which has never suffered an invasion by a foreign foe, is the number one target of the Soviet Union. We were reminded that we have a ring of steel encircling the iron curtain, composed of our multiple bases from which missiles may be fired in retaliation should we be attacked. To plug the long gaps between some of our foreign bases, our submarines now can pull up near the shores of any country, remain submerged, and still fire our missiles.

The great deterrent which keeps the Soviets from attacking our land is the fact that from these far-flung bases missiles could be fired which in thirty minutes would deal death to 150 million of their people. Yet, for all this gigantic strength, we have no sense of security and we are more agitated than ever by fear of what may come upon the earth. All of this brings home to our hearts the eternal truth that only through the cross can peace come to our planet.

The only ultimate peace is peace with God made possible by the wondrous cross.

> Bane and blessing, pain and pleasure,
> By the cross are sanctified;
> Peace is there that knows no measure,
> Joys that thro' all time abide.
>
> JOHN BOWRING

The death of the Redeemer is the pledge that he in whom all the fulness of the divine nature and power dwell will spare nothing to reconcile all men and all the universe to himself. "He that spared not his own Son, but delivered him up for us all, how shall he not with him also freely give us all things?" (Rom 8:32).

Now, what is the peace which the cross offers?

It is the opposite of spiritual estrangement. Men had drifted away from God, away from the homeland of the soul. There is no peace for a man who is away from home, only an aching emptiness, a haunting loneliness, and a ceaseless yearning for home. The peace which the cross offers is the peace of a hunter home from the hills, a sailor home from the seas, a warrior home from the battle.

It is the antithesis of hostility. When one is away from God, he is no longer right with God. He becomes hostile in his mind. Feverish, furious thoughts against God rage through his intellect. Moral madness sets in. He is opposed to the mind of God. Could anything be more pathetic than that finite man should be hostile toward the infinite God?

The peace which the cross brings is the opposite of the pangs of conscience which throb after some evil deed is done. Men do wrong because they are not right with God. Estrangement from God produces hostility of mind which results in corrupt living. Then it is that the conscience cries out for peace.

A few days ago, a beautiful, young university student, from a home of means and culture in a nearby city, went to her professor with her problem. He referred her to her pastor. The pastor marveled at the beauty and grace which God had given her, but saw mirrored in her eyes the haunting melancholia of an estranged and hostile soul.

With the open frankness of youth, she said that religion nauseated her, that she was quite above it. Furthermore, she declared that she felt quite at home at the fraternity parties, where liquor flowed freely, and in a dormitory room where she unabashedly declared that many of the girls practiced free love.

She then, with mock nonchalance, said, "The only thing troubling me is that these things don't trouble me."

Then her pastor said to her, "Young lady, the worst kind of trouble is being troubled over the feeling that you are no longer troubled about what should trouble you. For if this be true, it means that something unspeakably precious in you has died!

"The reason God forbids adultery (and when the word was spoken she bowed her head on the desk) is that you were not created for such a life. You can never be at peace in it. It brings only heartache and self-reproach. And no superficial veneer of sophistication can soothe the deep anguish of your soul. Only in purity is there peace."

Now, how is this peace provided? It is the result of reconciliation with God. When the barriers of estrangement, hostility, and corrupt living go down, then the heart is at rest.

"And you," wrote Paul, "he has now reconciled" (Col. 1:21-22, RSV). The aorist passive form of the verb emphasizes that reconciliation is an accomplished reality. Paul is again reminding the Colossians that they do not have to seek peace through angelic mediators. It has been accomplished. It is the supreme task of the church to declare the reconciliation that men may receive it.

It was accomplished by our Lord's death in his body of flesh.

All the powers which had produced man's hostility toward God—sin, death, law, and the demonic forces—were vanquished on the cross. Christ destroyed them all.

The battleground was the body of his flesh, for it was here, as Paul said, that sin did its work. He shed his blood and laid down his life in violent death in an amazing stroke of triumph over the mysterious powers which plague mankind. Thus he healed the discord between man and God and between man and man.

By yielding his own flesh in death, he put to death the area in which the sin principle operates. By his resurrection he entered his glorified body where sin and death can no more have dominion over him. He offers to lift us above the dominion of sin.

Look then at the result of reconciliation with God. True theology results in moral living. At his judgment seat he promises to present us "holy and blameless and irreproachable" (Col. 1:22, RSV). "Who shall lay any thing to the charge of God's elect?" (Rom. 8:33). No avenging angel will dare accuse the one whom God has reconciled unto himself. But there are conditions which must be met if the reconciliation is to be effective.

You must continue in the faith. There is but one true faith, once for all delivered to the saints. You must never alter it. It is the concrete, immutable deposit of God in history, unalterable and eternally fixed. You must grow in grace, but the roots of faith from which you grow will remain the same.

You must remain stable. To be stable means to have a sure foundation, a house built on a rock. "On Christ the solid Rock, I stand; all other ground is sinking sand."

You must be steadfast. To be steadfast means to persistently stand on the same rock. Persevering faith is the only kind of faith that saves. "He that endureth to the end shall be saved" (Matt. 10:22). There must be loyalty to Christ, for loss of loyalty, said Paul, means loss of hope. Peace is the gift of God's reconciling grace through the cross of the Redeemer.

13. The Significance of Suffering

Colossians 1:24

No one moves through life hopping from mountain peak to mountain peak of joy without at times descending into the vale of tears and the moors of suffering. The important question is: Do we allow our pain to purify and perfect us or to embitter and estrange us from God and man? As we sail the sea of life, we often encounter the storms.

It has been my good fortune to sail on two of the most magnificent ships that ever plowed the seas, the Queen Mary and the Queen Elizabeth. For sheer luxury, the older vessel, the Queen Mary, is to be desired. But the Queen Elizabeth has something which fascinates every sailor. She is the largest ship afloat. For years she rolled with the seas until four stabilizers were installed to help her keep an even keel.

One may be conducted into the engine rooms where those stabilizers are at work. There he will see four engines, each producing fifty thousand horsepower to drive the four propellers. Generators supplying enough electricity for a city and twelve boilers using one thousand tons of oil a day provide power and light for the massive vessel. The steering post and rudder assembly weigh 140 tons, yet are sensitive to the slightest touch of the wheel on the bridge. Most fascinating of all are the four stabilizers, giant fins, two on each side, fore and aft. Under the control of gyroscopes they are constantly adjusting to help keep the ship on an even keel as it moves through the many waters.

Because the waters of pain and anguish often pass over us and we are submerged into the great deep of suffering, we too need strong stabilizers for the soul. In this passage Paul mentions four:

The first is a constructive attitude toward suffering. Paul saw suffering, not as a catastrophe, but as the inevitable consequence of his labors for Christ. He lived in no unrealistic ivory tower. He looked through no rose-colored glasses. He saw the grim, hard battle of life. He remembered the words of his Master, "In the world ye shall have tribulation" (John 16:33). He knew that the Christian life is not walled around by an invulnerable fortress, that Christ gave no impregnable armor to any man. The Christian life is hard warfare to the very last, and we who fight are susceptible to mortal wounds.

Another stabilizer for the sea of suffering is in the strange joy that arises out of suffering. Paul knew this cry of earth's anguish. He wrote, "I rejoice in my sufferings for your sake" (Col. 1:24, RSV).

Who are the brightest, most joyous people you know? Are they those who are sheltered and petted and pampered and patronized? Is it not true that these are often the most cynical, ill-natured of souls, while those who have borne many a bitter pain have a quiet, gentle radiance and composure and compassion which only pain can produce.

Have you never stood at the bedside to watch one whom you dearly loved writhing in agony and wished that you might gather a part of their pain into your own body that they might know a few moments of comfort? This was the joy Paul knew. He said, "My suffering is for your sake."

Paul knew that the servant is not greater than his Lord. If a hostile world hounded the Master to his death, if the Lord of glory had to be laid in a tomb where for the first time in thirty-three years the cruel world ceased to torment him, what grounds has any Christian for believing that he will pass through life on flowery beds of ease? How poignant is the stanza we should sing with real comprehension:

> Must I be carried through the skies
> On flow'ry beds of ease,
> While others fought to win the prize
> And sailed thro' bloody seas?
>
> ISAAC WATTS

How unheroic is the peace-of-mind cult which offers a cheap facsimile of Christian faith. Instead Paul rejoices that he can bear a great part of the burden of the church which, without him, might be overwhelming for his fellow Christians.

Still another stabilizer is the realization that through suffering we enter into a deeper fellowship with Christ.

Paul, in his Philippian letter, had prayed that "I may know him, . . . and the fellowship of his sufferings" (Phil. 3:10). To know Christ involves entering into his anguish for a lost and sinful and suffering world. Of him Isaiah wrote, "In all their affliction he was afflicted" (Isa. 63:9). The word in the Septuagint is identical with the word used here for afflictions.

What did Paul mean when he wrote, "In my flesh I complete what is lacking in Christ's afflictions" (Col. 1:24, RSV)? He could not have been saying that there was anything lacking in Christ's atonement, for the purpose of the entire epistle is to present the adequacy of the gospel of Christ, that it requires no supplementing. Paul's thought is that the church is the extension of the incarnation of Christ so that the church's suffering—the sufferings of the people of God—are Christ's sufferings.

Paul so loved the church that he made the pain of every member his own. In a still higher sense the suffering of the church is the suffering of Christ, for the church is his body still bearing the pain of humanity.

The force of the prefix *ant* in *antanaplērō* bears this out. Paul stands in Christ's place to bear his suffering. The church also stands in Christ's place as his body to suffer with him. The apostle now himself bears the cross, drinks of the cup of which Christ drank, and is baptized with the baptism of pain with which he was baptized (Matt. 20:22-23).

The great stabilizer in times of suffering is the realization that we suffer for a great cause. Paul said, "In my flesh I complete what is lacking in Christ's afflictions for the sake of his body, that is, the church" (Col. 1:24, RSV).

The underlying thought is that those who afflict Christ's body, the church, Christ's people, afflict Christ. He who persecutes the church persecutes Christ. Who could know this better than Paul? Did not the risen Christ say to him, when he was the archpersecutor of the church, "Saul, Saul, why persecutest thou me?" (Acts 9:4). In persecuting Christ's people, Saul had persecuted Christ.

If we suffer in Christ's behalf, what a glory there is in that! The servant is not greater than his lord (John 13:16).

If you desire asylum and refuge from all pain, look not for it in the Christian faith; but if you desire the heroic life of the saints, you will find it here. What we need is the strong faith of the conquerors united with the conqueror from Calvary.

In a recent service in our church Dr. Walter Judd told about Dwight Eisenhower's faith and trust, as told to him by Mrs. Eisenhower. When Mr. Eisenhower is weary, worn, and worried when he lies down to sleep he says something like this: "Lord, I've done the best I can today, and I'm grateful for your help. Doubtless I muffed a few. You take over from here." "And then," says Mrs. Eisenhower, "he just turns over and goes to sleep."

There is a window through which you may see a city whose light is the Lamb (Rev. 21:23), whose glory is made possible by the suffering of the Lamb of God. Into that glory you may enter as you offer your sufferings to Christ as a part of the price of the redemption of this world.

The Christian concept of the church is that it is a fellowship of suffering in which each can bear the pain of all and all the pain of each for Christ's sake. We follow him who in all our afflictions is himself afflicted. Therefore, we may pray:

> Dear Master, in Whose life I see
> All that I long and fail to be;
> Let Thy clear light for ever shine
> To shame and guide this life of mine.
>
> Though what I dream and what I do
> In my poor days are always two,
> Help me, oppressed by things undone,
> O Thou, Whose dreams and deeds were one.
>
> JOHN HUNTER

14. The Mystery of the Gospel

Colossians 1:25-27

The world in which Paul preached thought of religion primarily in terms of strange esoteric mysteries. The multitude of cults were so secretive that they were called the mystery religions. For these religions worship had two parts. There were the public ceremonies which all might behold. Then there were certain esoteric doctrines which were carefully guarded under a seal of secrecy and divulged only to the chosen few. These secrets were so carefully guarded that even to this day scholars have not been able to say with certainty what these religions actually taught.

Over against this rigid exclusiveness, Paul comes to proclaim another kind of mystery, the mystery of the gospel which now is made known fully to all the world. Paul sees God working on a deep plan, a secret purpose which cannot be discerned by man's natural powers. If God's deep purpose is known, it must be revealed by God himself. God is not concerned with concealing himself but revealing himself.

For ages and generations this purpose has been concealed from the Gentiles, indeed from all men. This does not mean that God is a hostile deity delighting to conceal himself, from whom a Prometheus must steal the fire of heaven. It means rather that not even God could disclose his full nature and purpose until man reached the level of spiritual maturity to receive this revelation. The writer of Hebrews reminds us that God previously spoke in many and various ways until he finally spoke with finality through his Son (Heb. 1:1-2). At the first possible moment, God brought his Son into the world—even then his own received him not (John 1:11).

God's march across history has been an attempt to include all men. He called and made a covenant with Abraham, that through him all the families of earth might be blessed (Gen. 12:3). The Jews regarded themselves exclusively as God's people. Then the Jews had to be narrowed to a remnant of the faithful, and finally the remnant in which God dwelt was reduced to one. "God was in Christ" (2 Cor. 5:19). By his life, death, and resurrection he became the head of a redeemed humanity.

Now, Paul speaks of the mystery as the Word of God, the gospel itself. Look then at these things about this mystery.

First, it inheres in the universality of the gospel. Here is a totally new departure in religion. The gospel offers conditions which may be met by any man anywhere. It was Paul's high honor to proclaim for the first time the secret of the gospel. "To me, though I am the very least of all the saints, this grace was given, to preach to the Gentiles the unsearchable riches of Christ, and to make all men see what is the plan of the mystery hidden for ages in God who created all things" (Eph. 3:8-9, RSV). If the gospel were not for all men, who would ever have the brazen effrontery to believe that it was intended for him?

The heart of the mystery is the mystical union with Christ. "Christ in you, the hope of glory" (Col. 1:27). The hope centers in Christ who shows us what God intended humanity to be.

He wakes desires you never may forget;
  He shows you stars you never saw before;
  He makes you share with Him forevermore
The burden of the world's divine regret.

ALFRED TENNYSON

A. E. Whitham reminds us:

> If ever a personality had dynamic power, that personality was Jesus. His great words when spoken seemed to His followers to shake the very pillars of the universe; His great sayings go travelling down the ages like the wind in the trees, lifting and falling upon the heart of man like the harmonies of God; His joys appeared to those who beheld like a sun-washed hill-side after the darkness of ten thousand winters; His sorrows were like the travail of a God bringing new races to birth; His burden was as the burden of an Atlas; and His hopes were as glorious as the promises of God.[1]

It is not Christ among the Jews nor Christ among the Gentiles, but Christ in you which God has purposed through the ages. It is his actual living union with Christ, which transcends all human comprehension but which is nevertheless real through faith, which is God's open secret. As Pascal put it, "The heart has reasons which the reason knows not."

The mystery is God's disclosure. Man does not grasp it through inductive reasoning nor through superior powers of comprehension, for God does not make himself known purely through rational processes. He makes his personal encounter of grace and enables man to apprehend such a confrontation of the living God. This is the meaning of revelation.

This indwelling of Christ is the riches of the glory of this mystery "which is Christ in you, the hope of glory" (Col. 1:27). This is "the glory which shall be revealed in us" (Rom. 8:18). It is the future hope which is laid up in heaven but made real by the indwelling Christ. Just as the Holy Spirit is the "earnest of our inheritance" (Eph. 1:14), so also the Spirit, who makes real the presence of the living Christ, gives us through him the assurance of our heavenly inheritance. This brings the certainty of our salvation.

In the *Daisies of Nazareth,* Hugh MacMillan tells of a highland shepherd on a lonely moor who for many years had been infirm and blind. He was so crippled with rheumatism that he could not stir from his seat beside his lowly peat fire. One day a kindly visitor asked whether the hours which he spent in this manner were not weary and spoke of the blessedness of heaven. The old shepherd answered simply, "I know it well; I have been in heaven during the past ten years." He went on to explain to his visitor that since Jesus had entered his heart he had not felt the weariness he had before.

The mystery of the gospel which baffles this world is that Christ remains the only hope of our world. Modern men may feel that the case against Christ has been closed. When Emile Zola was condemned by his judges, his lawyer pointed to a crucifix and said, "Remember, gentlemen, that was once a closed case too, but it was opened again!"

The crucified Christ is looking down upon us with death in his bleeding hands and feet, but life is the light of his burning eyes, and demanding from us all—every individual man and woman—a choice between glory or force and wrath and fear. . . . He will not go away. I do not believe he will let us alone. He is going to drive us to a decision with his wounded hands. He will not let us have his world for a playground, a battlefield, a factory, or an empire any longer; we must give it to him—or else there will be darkness over all the earth from the sixth hour until the ninth—and that may be a thousand years.[2]

Notes

1. A. E. Whitham, *The Catholic Christ* (London: Hodder & Stoughton, Ltd., 1940), pp. 67-68. Used by permission.
2. From *The Best of Studdert-Kennedy* (London: Hodder & Stoughton, Ltd., 1947). Used by permission.

15. The Shepherd of the Stars

Colossians 1:28

The gospel of Christ can never truly be preached in this world until it is preached in all the world. The gospel includes a geographical dimension defined by our blessed Lord. "Go ye into all the world" (Mark 16:15). This command lay behind Paul's statement to the Colossians, "Him we proclaim, warning every man and teaching every man in all wisdom, that we may present every man mature in Christ" (Col. 1:28, RSV).

Paul knew that the gospel was not an esoteric secret discovered by, and reserved for, a few superior introverts. The gospel is for all this world and for all worlds.

In our day, when mankind stands trembling on the verge of an invasion into staggering dimensions of space, once more he lifts the question: Is the simple gospel of the Nazarene sufficient? Out yonder where mankind has never ventured, are we not likely to encounter much that will unsettle our faith?

The great question is not *what* lies out there but *who?* G. A. Studdert-Kennedy, the best loved chaplain of World War I, was walking through the night alone. Above him stretched the black dome of the heavens studded with a million stars. In the distance before him, he could hear the booming of the waves beating against the rock-bound coast. In the distance above him, he could hear the desolate cry of some lonely dove returning late to her nest. Suddenly, the question came crowding in upon him:

> When I stand feeling like a pigmy beneath the silent stars of a summer night, looking up at the mountains, listening to the sea, with the cry of the tortured ages of human history in my ears and the knowledge of the creative aeons in my mind, and ask as I am bound to ask, Why?[1]

Studdert-Kennedy said, as he raised the question and waited, the answer came, and came so clearly that it kept him steadfast through many a bitter hour of war. "There is no voice that answers except the voice of the Son of Man who died and rose again. Once I hear that Voice with the ears that can really hear, the pain in my mind begins to pass into peace."[2]

We need seasons of solitude when we get alone with the Great Alone and are so sure of his presence that from henceforth we know that even our most grim misfortunes are but the shade of his hand outstretched in everlasting mercy and love.

The question is, as we move through the space beyond, who moves before us? Paul said, "It is Christ! All things visible and invisible were created by him, are sustained by him, and will find their final goal in his redemption."

He is not only the shepherd of our souls, he is the shepherd of the stars. The ancient psalmist said, "He healeth the broken in heart, and bindeth up their wounds. He telleth the number of the stars; he calleth them all by their names" (Psalm 147:3-4). Only a star-counting God can stabilize the human soul in our age of space.

Have you ever thought of how often the Bible speaks of the stars? Joseph Gaer, in *How the Great Religions Began,* calls Christianity "the Star of the Purple East," and well he might for the Bible abounds in references to the stars. Job sees the morning stars singing together and the sons of God shouting for joy (Job

38:7). Balaam, the pagan prophet, said, "I shall see him, but not now: I shall behold him, but not nigh: there shall come a Star out of Jacob, and a Sceptre shall rise out of Israel" (Num. 24:17). The writer of the Judges saw the whole moral universe grounded in the same power that controls the stars, for said he, "The stars in their courses fought against Sisera" (Judg. 5:20).

Speaking of the coming of the Messiah, Israel declared, "The people that walked in darkness have seen a great light: they that dwell in the land of the shadow of death, upon them hath the light shined" (Isa. 9:2). It is small wonder then that when Jesus came, Zechariah said, "The dayspring from on high hath visited us" (Luke 1:78). He came to be a light to lighten the Gentiles and the glory of his people Israel (Luke 2:32). The last name Jesus called himself in the Bible was "the bright and morning star" (Rev. 22:16). You do not wonder then that this shepherd of the stars pulled as a magnet to his manger cradle the brightest star of the firmament.

Standing before this child of heaven, we see tiny hands not long enough to reach the huge heads of the cattle, yet these hands once flung out the sun, moon, and stars; we see tiny feet too weak to hold the infant body, now unable to take one step, yet they once trod the everlasting hills of heaven; a tiny mind which now knows not its mother's name, yet the moment before knew every secret of every human soul.

The God whose presence permeates all heaven and earth, in whom all things live and move and have their being, is now crowded into a remote corner of a cattle manger. A. E. Whitham said:

> I never see a night of stars without thinking that these are the jewels of His crown, which He cast aside when He took a crown of thorns. I never see a glorious sunset without thinking that it is the garment of His majesty, which He threw aside when He took the fustian of our laborious days. I never see a red rose without thinking

it is red with that redness because it has been dipped in the suffering heart of God.[3]

I see His blood upon the rose
  And in the stars the glory of His eyes,
His body gleams amid eternal snows,
  His tears fall from the skies.
. . . .
All pathways by His feet are worn,
  His strong heart stirs the ever-beating sea,
His crown of thorns is twined with every thorn,
  His cross is every tree.[4]

We look at the terrific humility of a God who came as a baby to Bethlehem and grew up to be a homeless man. We see him touch with healing hands bodies which now sleep under Syrian skies; we see him weep over cities that now have not one stone left on top of another; we see him shed tears the sun has mixed with the dews and rains of two thousand summers. We begin to know that there is nothing more impressive even in God than his humility. This shepherd of the stars is the shepherd of our souls.

"He healeth the broken in heart, and bindeth up their wounds. He telleth the number of the stars; he calleth them all by their names." He is not so lost among the stars that he is unmindful of every aching heart. As we pace the aisles of night in sleepless pain, he offers to bear our afflictions. As corrosive guilt crowds in upon us to suffocate our very souls and the curtains of mist come down over our eyes, only the Good Shepherd can console. Only one who has the cosmic dimensions of the divine in his soul can reach into the tangled past to forgive, move into the present to cleanse and transform, and into the future to hold us fast forever.

As we live on this remote, dying cinder, as it spins through space, the night is often dark and cold but Christ's presence is bright and his heart is warm.

The hands of Christ
  Seem very frail
For they were broken
  By a nail.

But only they
  Reach heaven at last
Whom these frail, broken
  Hands hold fast.

JOHN RICHARD MORELAND

Because Christ is the shepherd of the stars and of our world and all worlds, he is for all men. There are two areas where I believe we as Christians could work more vigorously. First, there is the college or university campus from which we must capture for Christ our leaders of tomorrow.

Do you know that we now have three hundred thousand foreign students on our campuses? They are from the finest families abroad. Too often we are unaware of their presence and we handle them as Mahatma Gandhi was handled. He was well on his way to becoming a Christian, was profoundly influenced by the Sermon on the Mount, until one day he visited a Christian church in South Africa. He was stopped at the door by a man who said that the church did not welcome Negroes. He told Gandhi that there were other churches for the likes of him. Gandhi vowed that evening that he would never enter a Christian church again. Had it not been for that one man who was so unchristian, India might be Christian today, led thereto by Gandhi.

Another major frontier we must invade is that composed of the southern Negro. The African chief still says to our missionaries, "Don't bother to come over here to preach the fatherhood of God until you practice the brotherhood of man at home!" Actions speak louder than words.

Little Mary loved her father but she was having trouble with her brother. When her father came home, she ran to meet him, put her arms about his neck and looking over his shoulder, she stuck out her tongue at her brother. Her father said, "Mary, take down your arms. You can't love your father and stick out your tongue at your brother."

Still are there multitudes so blinded by prejudice that they can even pretend to do mission work and still consider the Negro the Almighty's major blunder. I shall never forget playing ball during my childhood on a diamond on our city's east side. One ball game was suddenly halted by policemen chasing a Negro boy across the diamond. He had stolen something from a neighborhood grocery store and they were in hot pursuit. At length the boy fell exhausted to the ground. I can still hear the sickening thud of the policeman's billy against the helpless and defenseless head of the Negro child and the mocking laughter of the white men crying, "You can't hurt a Negro's head."

Against this mockery of human dignity rolls down the indictment of heaven. God "hath made of one blood all nations of men for to dwell on all the face of the earth" (Acts 17:26). We are going to have to learn to live together in this world or we are not going to live in it at all.

Only one-fifth of the world's population is white. We are the minority. We had better learn to love Martel's aria from the opera *Troubled Island:*

I dream a world where men
  No other man will scorn,
Where love will bless the earth
  And peace their path adorn.

. . . .

A world I dream where black or white,
  Whatever race you be,
Will share the bounties of the earth
  And every man be free. . . .[5]

Notes

1. *The Best of Studdert-Kennedy, op. cit.,* p. 153.
2. *Ibid.*
3. Whitham, *op. cit.,* pp. 88-89.
4. Joseph Mary Plunkett, "I See His Blood Upon the Rose" (Dublin, Ireland: The Talbot Press Limited). Used by permission.
5. Langston Hughes, "I Dream a World," from the opera libretto *Troubled Island* (New York: Leeds Music Corporation, 1949). Used by permission.

16. When Christ Builds the Church

Colossians 2:1-7

By the lifting power of the Holy Spirit the apostle Paul climbed centuries ahead of the church to show us clearly what God intended the church to be. In the passage before us you see the strong concern of Paul for the church. Here is the passionate pleading of a man of prayer. His was one of the giant intellects of the ages; yet this did not prevent his emotions from breaking through, for he writes, "I wish you could understand how deep is my anxiety for you" (Col. 2:1, Phillips). I want you to know what a struggle I am having on your behalf. Paul literally carried this church in his heart.

In the closing verse of the first chapter, he declared, "For this I toil, striving with all the energy which he mightily inspires within me" (Col. 1:29, RSV). Here he takes an illustration, as he often does, from the athletic games. He thinks of himself as taking part in a great contest, yet the strength he puts forth is not his own. A divine power has taken possession of him and raises him above himself. The word for energy is one of the characteristic words of Paul and reflects his idea that through faith in Christ a man connects his life with higher forces which support his own endeavor.

The sense of carrying other people in his heart drained the apostle's energy; yet Christ continued to give the necessary energy. Paul can carry the strain of the ministry only because Christ provides the energy. And in this energy he struggles even from his prison cell for the church.

Paul's desire for the church is "that their hearts might be comforted" (Col. 2:2). He sees the church as a source of ceaseless encouragement. It is not comfort in the sense of solace for which Paul yearns, nor is it encouragement in the sense of cheering words or flattering phrases. Rather, it is the encouragement that comes from divine reinforcement. The word *paralēthōsin* means to call to one's side. It means that a power not their own has come to confirm their affectionate loyalty to Christ.

He desires the church to be a home made up of loving hearts, hearts "being knit together in love" (Col. 2:2). Thus Paul prays for the church that she may find out more and more how strong are the bonds of Christian love.

The only evidence that the love of God has come through to his people is in their love one for another. Jesus said: "A new commandment I give unto you, That ye love one another; as I have loved you, that ye also love one another. By this shall all men know that ye are my disciples, if ye have love one to another" (John 13:34-35).

It is love alone which will hold the church together when divisive forces without and within are seeking to disrupt her fellowship. When a Christian congregation is interlocked in love no false teacher can break those bonds of love. Neither can any enemy of Christ prevail against the strong love of God which is the cohesive power which holds the church together.

Paul longs for the church to be a maturing family. "As therefore you received Christ Jesus the Lord, so live in him, rooted and built up in him and established in the faith" (Col. 2:6-7, RSV). "Grow out of Him as a plant grows out of the soil it is planted in, becoming more and more sure of your 'ground,' and your lives will overflow with joy and thankfulness" (Col. 2:6-7, Phillips).

The major reason for so much mental, emotional, and spiritual immaturity in our world is that we have deserted the only soil in which we may grow. We are what Elton Trueblood calls a "cut flower civilization." Christ is the soil for mental growth, "For it is in Him, and in Him alone, that men will find all the treasures of wisdom and knowledge" (Col. 2:3, Phillips).

The difference between the wisdom of the false teachers and that in Christ is that the false wisdom was hidden from view but it was not inexhaustible. When these secrets were presented to men they soon could be completely mastered. But no man has yet fully comprehended Christ. This is the difference between a dead and a living church. The dead church thinks it has already understood and performed the will and work of God. The living church realizes she is only beginning to discover the boundless depths of the wisdom of God in Christ. After his great discovery, Isaac Newton said that he felt like a child playing with pebbles on the shore while a great ocean of truth lay open before him.

Paul, near the end of his life, could still pray that he might know Christ. He could say with unshakable confidence, "I know whom I have believed" (2 Tim. 1:12), but he was never so naïve as to feel that he had comprehended all that there was in Christ. This is the reason we believe the church must continue to teach every man in all wisdom, that we may present every man mature in Christ. This is the reason the most useful servants of Christ continue to learn of him to the end of life. This is the reason the late John R. Sampey, great Hebrew scholar and president of the Southern Baptist Theological Seminary, was enrolled in a layman's study group of his church when he was past eighty years of age.

Christ is the soil in which emotional maturity is developed. Nothing is more essential to emotional health than a sense of security and assurance. Therefore, Paul prays that these Christians of Colossae might "grow more certain in your knowledge and more sure in your grasp of God" (Col. 2:2, Phillips).

Paul sees the church also as a disciplined army. He speaks of the "order, and the steadfastness of your faith in Christ" (Col. 2:5). Both of these are military terms. *Taxis* (order) means a rank or an ordered arrangement. He sees the church standing in military arrangement, rank upon rank, every man in his own place, alert and responsive to the word of command.

Stereōma means a solid bulwark, an immovable phalanx. William Barclay says: "It describes an army set out in an unbreakable square, solidly immovable against the shock of the charge of the enemy. Within the church there should be a disciplined . . . body of troops."[1]

Paul declares, "For though I am a long way from you in body, in spirit I am by your side, watching like a proud father the solid steadfastness of your faith in Christ" (Col. 2:5, Phillips). Many use Paul's statement to say, "I can't be at church but I'll be with you in spirit." They forget that Paul was in prison at this time.

Leslie D. Weatherhead tells that the tiny church of St. Ennadoc stood in a lovely spot among the sand hills in Cornwall. People worshiped there and offered God their simple vows. Slowly attendance fell until one Sunday the door was not opened. Sand blowing against the building mounted higher and higher till only the stony finger of the spire remained to remind men and women of vows now ruined, prayers now silent, and hope now dead.[2]

When Christ builds the church he expects his followers to attend in body whenever possible. It is not enough to attend in spirit only.

Notes

1. Barclay, *op. cit.,* p. 158.
2. Wallis, *op. cit.,* p. 70.

17. Low Use of High Religion

Colossians 2:8

The depth of human depravity is most graphically revealed in the fact that men will use the most precious things of life for very wicked purposes. Men have taken the most beautiful places of earth and reduced them to ugliness. Between the Euphrates and the Tigris rivers, we are told, there once stood a Garden of Eden. Men plundered it until its rivers dried up and it became a barren desert. Once the valley of the Nile was the most fertile place on earth, a place of wondrous productivity and creativity, but now it is a barren waste. What men have done in the natural realm, they have also done in the spiritual realm.

In Colossae there were men whose hearts were set on plundering the souls of men and undermining the Christian church by deliberately deluding her members. The Greek verb is very rare and graphic. It pictures false teachers as "men stealers" who entrap innocent souls into slavery. "See to it," says Paul, "that no one makes a prey of you" (Col. 2:8, RSV). One of the most pathetic things of earth is to see a man whose very soul is taking refuge in a religion which is nothing more than a vain delusion.

One sure means of detecting false religion is that it is concerned with plundering people, enslaving them in a system instead of respecting the dignity and freedom of the human soul.

When any religion seeks to manipulate men rather than to minister to them, it is not the religion of the Lord Christ. Nothing so marked his ministry and teaching as his emphasis on the sovereign dignity of human personality. If we believe what he taught, we will know that a human being has worth and value, not because the Constitution of our country says so nor because our religious creed says so, but because God made him and there will never be another like him.

Years ago in the womb of your mother were two cells. In these cells were the length of your arm, the droop of your shoulder, the color of your hair, the number of your teeth, and the intricacy of your nervous system.

The marvel of it all is that from the beginning of time, with all the millions and billions of men on earth, there has never been another like you. This is true experientially just as it is physically. From the beginning of time no human being has had the reservoir of memory you have. This means that no individual can make the contribution that you can make in the solution of life's problems. Because God has given you the dignity of a unique personality, the foremost task of the Christian church is to bring into actuality your unique potentiality.

It is not expected of you that the church should be allowed to squeeze you into a mold. You are unique. The church cannot expect you to do what any other has done. This would only doom the work of the church to a ministry of mediocrity. The church, if it is true to God's creative purpose for you, must enable you to make the maximum of your own unique personality, your own reservoir of memory, and your own background of experience.

The church as a group can accomplish what no individual can but only as she leaves each member to make his unique contribution. No church is at her best if she is not cultivating the God-given uniqueness of each member.

True religion has no unscrupulous designs to use men to achieve arbitrary man-made goals. It is concerned solely that men may be rooted and grounded in the truth of Christ.

Paul sees gratitude as the certain sign of spiritual health. When men are grateful for the truth made plain in Christ, they are not strongly tempted to grasp the falsehood of human traditions.

These false teachers were attempting to plunder the souls of men by distorting the original gospel. They were presuming to enhance the gospel by an intriguing philosophy which appealed to the pride of men who delighted to call themselves intellectuals.

Paul called their philosophy an empty deceit. It was pseudo-philosophy. Now it was not that Paul did not appreciate philosophy as an honest attempt to interpret the great mysteries of life in a rational way. Paul himself was a philosopher. His profound discourse in the previous chapter concerning the relationship of Christ to the cosmos (Col. 1:15-20) is evidence of his gigantic intellect. Paul is here refuting empty speculation which misguided teachers were dignifying with the name philosophy.

When Paul warned the church, "Beware lest any man spoil you through philosophy and vain deceit" (Col. 2:8), he was not talking about two separate things, but one. He meant that kind of philosophy which is empty deceit. It is true that at times Paul does not believe that the tree of knowledge is the tree of life. He knew that when God measures a man, he puts the tape around the heart instead of the head; yet he never disparaged philosophy when it meant clear thinking.

T. R. Glover said, "Christians conquered the pagan world because the Christian outlived, outthought and outdied the pagan."[1] Paul could outthink the pagan world. He felt it very important to know that Christianity has nothing to fear from the camp of the outside world in the realm of truth.

These false philosophers were attempting to harmonize the Christian faith with the terms and concepts of the current philosophy and perhaps unconsciously were accommodating Christianity to what the world had before Christ came. For them Christ was not the final authority. The current philosophy sat on the judgment seat, causing men to squeeze Christianity into a rational mold. They could not realize what John Locke later emphasized, that while Christianity is never against reason, it is always above reason; that the truth of Christ is something that is never comprehended by men until they are, first of all, apprehended by Christ.

Notes

1. Quoted in Wallis, *op. cit.*, p. 67.

18. Above All Angels

Colossians 2:9

Concerning Jesus Christ, Paul says that he is the head of all rule and authority (Col. 2:9). He is above all the orders of the angels.

How strange and archaic it seems to the modern mind for man to talk about angels! We want something practical, something our minds can comprehend, even when we go to church. We want nothing to do with the eerie, invisible realm. We will leave that to the spiritualists.

We want something to match the grim, hard circumstances in which we beat out life's little day. We want a down-to-earth religion. We have no time for the world of mystery and wonder. Now, the most down-to-earth religion in our world is communism. The economic determinism of Karl Marx equates a classless society on earth with the kingdom of God. In our generation it has swept one-third of the world's population behind the iron and bamboo curtains.

Now, I want to suggest that the major reason Americans are so weary, empty, and bored today is because we have made our religion too practical. Our lingering emptiness and boredom is the result of having brought God down to our own level. We need communion with someone above the angels. Man's prideful arrogance has reduced religion to the realm of magic in which he vainly believes that he has a means of manipulating the Almighty. Unless we believe that God is high and holy and infinitely above us, worship of him is impossible.

The Mackerel Plaza is the satirical story of a modern minister seeking the maximum faith that the facts of life and the truth of the universe will permit an honest man. He is a man determined to believe without going back to the nursery. Toward the end of the book he tells of various congregations of his town organizing prayer meetings to pray for rain. Mackerel cynically calls these prayer meetings "rain dances" and will have nothing to do with them. Then, by coincidence or otherwise, on the night of the prayer meeting a torrential rain came down.

Mackerel is disturbed no end, not because he suddenly finds that God answers prayer, but he deeply resents the thought that God, as he puts it, has been pushed about by all the bores, dullards, and bigots in town. He feels that if that is the lot God gives aid and comfort to, so be it. But he cannot worship him. He can believe in him, but he cannot worship him.

Thinking people find this a great problem. Religion, for so many, seems to move in the realm of magic where softheaded answers are given to hardheaded questions. This makes it utterly imperative that men who want to make life count for the things that matter most, and who are scrupulously honest, distinguish between religion and magic. Religion is man's attempt to know, and his endeavor to do, the will of God. Magic is the endeavor to bend the forces beyond us to do our own bidding.

In Colossae the false teachers were seeking to mingle magic with religion—to cause Christians to intermingle their theology with their established astrology. These believed that a man's destiny was written in the stars. Even to this day there are people who have their horoscopes cast. This kind of astrological determinism would obviously undermine the Christian concept of freedom and its corresponding sense of moral responsibility. It was a blind fatalism which said, "Ally yourself with the elemental spirits of the universe for they alone control your destiny." Paul said that not by placating the hostile spirits in the heights can man come into the fulness of life but by entering into Christ. In him all fulness of life dwells.

Paul called his followers to give their supreme allegiance to a high religion which paid worship to a God who is above all angels. "He is the head of all rule and authority." How strange it is that men should feel that believing in a high and sovereign God is an unrealistic flight from reality. It is all right to build castles in the air, provided we put foundations under them. Christ came into the world to give concrete foundations to our knowledge of God. The Most High was born in lowly humility to lay hold on the humblest of us and to lift us into the communion of him whose glory is written above the heavens.

Men who are honest with themselves know that only a great, all-knowing being is worthy of their worship. All we have seen should cause us to trust the Creator for all we have not seen. God is moving on to the fulfilment of some glorious purpose which all the nuclear energy on this earth, in the hands of foolish men, will not finally thwart. God is more than a creator bringing a world into being. He is a Father who trains, plans, nurtures, educates, loves, and guides us into a full realization of our capacities.

Since God is our Father, he does not cast us off even in times of our extreme hostility. When man is blinded by bewildering grief, he often strikes out at God. But even still, God loves him until his blind eyes are opened. In truth, there is more religious faith in honest rebellion against God than there is in superficial, sentimental, blind submission to God.

John B. Coburn demonstrates this in his account of a young father who sat grim-faced through the funeral of his four-year-old son who had died of polio:

As he listened to the words, "I know that my Redeemer liveth," he kept murmuring under his breath: "God, I'll get back at you for this. I'll get back at you for this." This was the first honest conversation he had ever had with God. Later he commented, "That was a foolish thing to say, I suppose. How could I ever get back at God?" Yet, it was honest and it kept the relationship with God open. That was the way I felt, and it was right to clear the atmosphere and get it all off my chest. For then I gradually came to myself and saw that death does have to go into some final framework and only God can absorb it. I read and reread all those experiences of men suffering before God, especially Job, and in time his sentiments became mine, or almost mine. I know now that my Redeemer does live, and I don't think I should know it, down deep inside, if I hadn't been mad at my Redeemer once—and said so."[1]

Here was a man who began his relationship with God out of his anger over the hard, unfair circumstances of life. We must be encouraged to go to the depths of our feelings about God and through our honesty let God come through to us.

Only through worship of a high God can we have adequate resources for life. Only a God above all angels is adequate for our age of space. This high God must give us moral and spiritual altitude. Billy Graham has said:

> . . . America can rise no higher than the individuals who walk her streets, conduct her business, teach her young people, make her homes and attend her churches. It is these individuals who must be changed. . . . It was to make new men and women that Christ came into the world.[2]

In Christ is all the fulness of the Godhead bodily. This means all his power is pledged to see us through. He is ever seeking to come to us. All of our search for God is but our response to his search for us.

In "The Explorer" Kipling has this line: "Anybody might have found it, but—His whisper came to me!"[3] The faintest whisper to your soul is God's voice, if you will only listen. Too often we are like the king in Shaw's *Saint Joan*. The king was utterly outraged because Saint Joan heard the voice of God telling her what she should do and he did not hear it. He demanded to know why the voices did not come to him. She replied simply that it was because he was not listening.

Elisha's story in its mighty symbols still speaks to us (2 Kings 6:8-23). Elisha and his servant were pursued by the king of Assyria. They were discovered in Dothan. Then the Syrian monarch sent hosts of horses and chariots and surrounded the city. Early in the morning the servant of the man of God arose before his master and saw that the enemy had surrounded them. Frantically, he called to Elisha, "Alas, my master! how shall we do?"

Like a benediction from God himself came Elisha's answer: "Fear not: for they that be with us are more than they that be with them." Then he asked God to open the young man's eyes that he might see the resources of God. Then his eyes were opened and he saw. "And, behold, the mountain was full of horses and chariots of fire round about Elisha."

Ours is such a pale counterfeit of Elisha's faith. We have lost our confidence. Why not in these moments ask God to give us such an experience so that we too might be confident that even pain, duty, and death itself are gates into a new life into which at any moment we may, by the grace of God, pass.

Notes

1. Quoted in William Summerscales, "In Jesus' Name," *Pulpit Digest*, XLI (September, 1960), 80. Used by permission.
2. Billy Graham, "Men Must Be Changed Before a Nation Can," *Life*, XLVIII (June 6, 1960), 126. Used by permission.
3. Rudyard Kipling, "The Explorer," from *The Five Nations* (New York: Doubleday & Co., Inc., 1903). Reprinted by permission.

19. Pictures of Forgiveness

Colossians 2:13-15

G. K. Chesterton admonishes us not to believe anything which cannot be presented in colored pictures. It is true that the great centralities of the Christian faith are best seen in pictures, not in logical argument. Our blessed Lord spoke in pictorial language. So did Paul, our Lord's most graphic interpreter. In Colossians 2:13-15, Paul portrays forgiveness in five vivid scenes.

First, forgiveness brings resurrection of life. "You, who were dead in trespasses . . . God made alive together with him, having forgiven us all our trespasses" (Col. 2:13, RSV).

Life is possible only in union with Christ. "In him we live, and move, and have our being" (Acts 17:28). Sin breaks the union with Christ and banishes men to the realm of death where they are utterly powerless to reform or restore the lost relationship. Dead men cannot atone for their sins, cannot make amends, cannot lift themselves back to God. Every time man yields to temptation he is giving the forces of death the right of way in his life.

Only Christ can liberate us from the power of death and lift us back into life. This he does by forgiving our sins. He invites all men to receive forgiveness at his hand. Even the uncircumcised Gentiles who have no covenant with God are not excluded. Jesus came not primarily to make bad men good but dead men live.

Forgiveness also cancelled the bond which stood against us. Colossians 2:14 reads, "[Jesus Christ] Blotting out the handwriting of ordinances that was against us." All the debts that were charged against us have now been cancelled.

Cheirographon literally signified an autograph. It was used to describe a note which a debtor signed acknowledging his indebtedness. It was the ancient counterpart of our modern IOU. Paul saw man's sins written in the accounts of God.

The writer of Revelation speaks of the book of works. "And I saw the dead, small and great, stand before God; and the books were opened: and another book was opened, which is the book of life: and the dead were judged out of those things which were written in the books, according to their works" (Rev. 20:12).

Paul sees a charge account which men have admitted signing but cannot pay. Now it is blotted out forever by forgiveness.

God's marvelous mercy is revealed in the Greek verb *exaleiphein,* meaning "blotted out." Ancient accounts were kept either on papyrus which was composed of the pith of the bulrush or vellum made from the skins of animals. These were used over and over as we would use a chalk slate. At that time the ink contained no acid and did not, therefore, bite into the paper. To save paper the ancient scribe would simply take a sponge and erase the ink which lay on the surface. Now, when Paul said that God blotted out our sins by his forgiveness, he meant that he erased them without leaving a trace of our guilt in his sight.

The pathetic thing about sin for the unforgiven is that he becomes obsessed with it. As David of old, we cry, "My sin is ever before me" (Psalm 51:3). We can see nothing in its proper perspective, for we look through the dark veil of sin. Paul tells us God has put our sin out of his sight; now we must do likewise. One of the great problems in forgiveness is not that God will not forgive but that man in his prideful arrogance will not forgive himself. He feels that he must sit in harsher judgment upon himself even than

God would practice. Paul would have us know that if God has put our sins out of his sight, we ought also to forgive ourselves and cease thinking of our past transgressions.

Perhaps even more is involved in this picture. This bond which Christ has cancelled includes the law which has condemned man. The Colossian heresy probably included the insistence that the Jewish law was the means by which man's fellowship with God was maintained. Paul says that by the grace of God even the law has been abolished. Christ is the law of God incarnate. John Calvin once said: "The sacrificial ritual in Judaism implies the fact of guilt. As long as you have these ordinances, you have the memory of guilt. To take away the memory of guilt, the ordinances must be taken away."

Still is it true, just as it was in Colossae, that men are constantly seeking to smother the spontaneity of the Christian gospel by reintroducing ancient rituals, rules, and regulations. Paul said that these have been swept away forever, for they are nailed to his cross.

The aorist form of the verb translated "nailed" signifies a definite act done once for all. Paul changes metaphors to reinforce the truth. He has blotted out the indictment. Now he nails it to his cross. Some see in this an ancient custom of driving a nail through a document to cancel it. More probably it had to do with the nailing of the indictment to the cross of a criminal. Paul sees the very indictment against our being crucified with Christ so that we are no longer under the law but under grace.

> Free from the law, O happy condition,
> Jesus hath bled, and there is remission;
> Cursed by the law and bruised by the fall
> Grace hath redeemed us once for all.
>
> P. P. Bliss

Even the forces which superintended the law have now been

stripped of their powers and authorities. "He disarmed the principalities and powers and made a public example of them, triumphing over them in him" (Col. 2:15, RSV).

The Jews believed that the law was ordained by angels. They saw their ordinances as being closely connected with the principalities and powers. Hebrews 2:2 speaks of the word spoken by angels. When Paul refers to the law in this passage, he is thinking not of the moral law but of the ceremonial law which Christ fulfilled and which must not be reimposed on his people.

The people in Colossae thought of the principalities and powers as being responsible for all the demon-possessed on earth and all the evil on earth. They were often hostile toward men. Christ has now disarmed them, as stripping the weapons from a conquered enemy. They can no longer harm those whom Christ has surrounded with his strong redeeming grace. By his forgiveness, Christ has liberated men from all evil forces which would pull them down.

Christ is the cosmic conqueror who has vanquished every enemy of man. Man's spiritual foes have been publicly put to shame.

The Roman general would parade through the street leading his captives before him. So said Paul, "Christ moved through this universe with every power which would do harm to the souls of men trailing behind him vanquished forever."

In 2 Corinthians 2:14, Paul wrote, "Thanks be to God, who in Christ always leads us in triumph, and through us spreads the fragrance of the knowledge of him everywhere" (RSV). This does not mean that we are triumphant but that we are trophies of the conqueror's power. We are captives behind the triumphant chariot of Christ. God's victory over human life is more than the victory of human life.

Through the cross, he leads even the redeemed captive in his triumphal train. The cross is now the victor's chariot. Even the accursed cross has been redeemed. Calvin said that there is no tribunal so magnificent, no chariot so splendid as is the gallows on which Christ subdued Satan and his cohorts. The death of Christ itself was essentially victory. It is not that his death was turned into victory. His death itself was victory. "O death, where is thy sting? O grave, where is thy victory?" (1 Cor. 15:55).

H. G. Wells rightly protests against the crucifix. If we must have a crucifix, let us have one not downcast but one with eyes fixed resolutely on the skies with the defeated powers beneath his feet. This is not Jesus bowing submissively but Christ wielding the hammer, shouting, "No man takes my life!" He refused the anesthetic. He remained active. This man is master even on the cross. He is, therefore, the master of all that masters you.

"Thanks be to God, which giveth us the victory through our Lord Jesus Christ" (1 Cor. 15:57).

Through him we too may ride in the conqueror's chariot, bound to him forever by his forgiving grace. This is the only true freedom.

Make me a captive, Lord,
  And then I shall be free;
Force me to render up my sword,
  And I shall conqueror be.
I sink in life's alarms
  When by myself I stand;
Imprison me within Thine arms,
  And strong shall be my hand.

. . . .

My power is faint and low
  Till I have learned to serve:
It wants the needed fire to glow,
  It wants the breeze to nerve;
It cannot drive the world
  Until itself be driven;
Its flag can only be unfurled
  When Thou shalt breathe from heaven.

My will is not my own
  Till Thou hast made it Thine;
If it would reach a monarch's throne
  It must its crown resign:
It only stands unbent
  Amid the clashing strife,
When on Thy bosom it has leant
  And found in Thee its life.

George Matheson

20. Beyond the Shadows

Colossians 2:16-23

It is the strong temptation of youth to say, "We want the good life but why do we need religion?" Karl H. A. Rest gives the answer:

Ethics without religion has little power to endure. The French Revolution began by striking the idealistic notes of liberty, equality, and fraternity; but it was no deeper than its own idealism. Its power for good was soon exhausted, and it broke loose in uncontrolled violence. When man has nothing more to rely upon than his own spirit, his goodness turns sour. He needs divine support. He lives most meaningfully when he responds to the gracious overtures of God.[1]

You cannot live on the highest level without being certain about some things. In one of our colleges, the Dean's office discovered that a woman for the last four years had elected the same course in algebra, although she had passed it the first time. The Dean wrote for an explanation. The woman replied: "I am so tired of arguing with my neighbors about everything in the world that I wanted to study something I couldn't argue about." Urgent human hunger was speaking then. Wanted—something, even mathematics, that in this perishable world is secure and constant.

In this changing world you must be sure of something that never changes, or better, of someone who never changes. Here he is: "Jesus Christ the same yesterday, and to day, and for ever" (Heb. 13:8).

The trouble with much of our religion is that it is as uncertain and insubstantial as shadows. Paul saw the Colossian teachers attempting to overshadow the fulness of the light of God that came in Christ by re-establishing rituals and regulations which were shadowy portrayals of the coming of Christ. With the coming of his light, these should have vanished from the scene because they had served their purpose.

Paul warned the congregation, "Let no man therefore judge you in meat, or in drink, or in respect of an holyday, or of the new moon, or of the sabbath days" (Col. 2:16). How easy it is for us to be more concerned about the judgment of men than the deeper judgment of God. The only measure by which man can judge us is composed of the regulations which man has made. Only God can see the heart and judge the motives of men.

Even those ceremonials which have become a part of the Christian way may become a substitute for the reality they represent. It is a good thing to observe Christmas but not as a substitute for the birth of the Christ in your own heart. It is a good thing to celebrate Easter but not as a substitute for the resurrection of life in which we are lifted up with Christ in heavenly places. These great Christian ceremonials are in no wise Christian unless they keep before us the reality of Jesus Christ. Only in Christ is there the substance of religion. Outward ceremonies and regulations are but shadows.

Often we interpret religion solely in terms of irksome rules. Moffatt, therefore, translates this passage, "Let no one lay down rules for you as he pleases." The reason many delight in a religion of rules is because it is much easier to submit to rules than it is to die to self.

Conformity to rules is often a rationalization for allowing self to remain on the throne. Submission to rules only drives that which you are trying to conquer deeper into the subconscious realm of life. Such does not free a man from fleshly lusts. Christ came to free us from the tyranny of petty rules by giving us a pattern which no code, however lengthy, could adequately define and by giving us a new heart empowered to follow him.

The keeping of rules is coupled by Paul with a false sense of humility, which was expressed in the worship of angels rather than going directly to God in Christ. This mock humility caused men to refrain from standing before God for themselves.

Worshiping secondary mediators rather than God in Christ leads a man to substitute his own speculation for the truth of God. He takes his stand on visions. He trusts his intellectual ability rather than the revealed truth of God. "He," said Paul, "is treading on the void of air." By intruding into things he has not seen he is as an acrobat, stepping on emptiness in a balancing feat.

This mock self-abasement and spurious humility leads to deadly pride. All self-conscious humility is fraudulent. It makes a man proud of his humility. It causes him to be puffed up without reason by his fleshly mind.

Paul, therefore, entreated them: "Let no man beguile you or disqualify you, as the umpire would rule you ineligible for the reward." "I always tell my young people, 'walk proudly in the light,' " says Mary MacLeod Bethune, Negro educator and founder of Bethune-Cookman College. "Faith ought not to be a puny thing. If we believe, we should believe like giants. I wish this blessing for my students and for American youth everywhere: 'May God give you not peace but glory!' "[2]

The feeling of superiority to others, even in the realm of humility, is the worst form of the sins of the flesh. Paul did not interpret the sins of the flesh simply in terms of the baser iniquities. He calls idolatry, strife, jealousy, rivalry (Gal. 5:20) also sins of the flesh. A brother-berating, ego-inflating attitude is a sin of the flesh.

In the ancient world Hippocrates taught that all the vital forces of life flow from the head. Life could not go on if the body were separated from the head. Christ is the head. To substitute anything in our religious experience for him is to commit spiritual suicide. What these Colossians were advocating as progress was actually retrogression into the shadowland in which humanity groped before the star shone over Bethlehem.

There is only one way to get beyond the shadows into the serene light of reality and that is to die with Christ in full surrender to him. All earthly ordinances will cease to be important. You will be lifted into the freedom of the new life of those who delight to walk the high road with Christ. There must be constant recommittal and surrender to Christ.

A sixteen year old girl came to her pastor somewhat troubled about the matter of her consecration. "Why do I have to make so many new consecrations?" she inquired, just a bit impatiently. "I did it at the youth camp a year ago and again this summer, and then tonight in the young people's meeting we were called upon to put everything on the altar again. Why isn't once enough?" "Well, it is just a little like Christopher Columbus' voyages to the New World," the preacher replied. "You remember that when he finally arrived at the tiny little island of San Salvador in 1492, he raised the flag of his monarchs, Ferdinand and Isabella, and claimed the land in the name of Spain. Then when he went on to Cuba, he did the same thing again. On each voyage, when he arrived at a new spot, he made a new dedication. Life is a little like that if we are Christians."[3]

He who has tasted the good life in Christ does not major on physical diets which say, "Touch not, taste not, handle not." These things are as perishable as the doctrines of men which describe them. To major on petty regulations is to return to slavery, repudiating the freedom with which Christ hath set you free.

The asceticism urged by the Colossian teachers was actually

involved in an irreconcilable contradiction. It taught basically that the body is evil. Two conclusions could, therefore, be drawn from this premise, either of which would be equally valid.

First, if the body is essentially evil, man could not be responsible for it. It would not, therefore, make any difference what he did with it. He could be justified in using it according to its very nature, to glut it or debauch it.

Second, if the body is evil, we must keep it down and suppress its natural appetites. Paul would have nothing to do with this rigid asceticism, for he would not agree with the premise. Rather did he believe that the body was created of God and would one day share in his total redemption, even in the resurrection. He did say, "But I keep under my body, and bring it into subjection" (1 Cor. 9:27). Yet, there he was simply acknowledging that the body is the area where the sin principle operates. What really matters is whether or not we have adequate spiritual resources to control the body and direct it to the high service of God. Only the indwelling Christ can supply these resources.

Notes

1. Quoted in Charles L. Wallis (ed.), *Speakers' Illustrations for Special Days* (New York: Abingdon Press, 1956), pp. 131-32. Used by permission.
2. *Ibid.*, pp. 118-19. Copyrighted by Reader's Digest, Inc., Pleasantville, New York. Used by permission.
3. Roy L. Smith, *Stewardship Studies* (New York: Abingdon Press, 1954). Used by permission.

21. The Accent on Life

Colossians 3:1-4

Robert W. Burns tells of standing on a balcony at England's Warwick Castle, overlooking one of the most beautiful scenes on earth. There at the base of the castle was the winding river; next to the river were lovely green fields. Next to the fields there were large squares of the beautiful yellow of the mustard plant; and stretching off into the distant hills, one after the other, were scenes of breath-taking beauty. Beside him stood one of those tourists who has often been an embarrassment to this country. He looked down at the river and his sole comment on all that loveliness was that it was terrible that there was such scum on the river. Although he thought he was judging the landscape, he really was judging himself.

So many still regard the religion of the great Redeemer in a negative attitude. They behold it as a dreary discipline which man should improve or blandly think of it as one of the multiple implements which a man may or may not choose for his self-improvement. But I want to tell you that Christianity has nothing to do with any of that. Christianity has the accent on life, not on the dreary discipline which ends in death.

Paul comes in this passage to draw a contrast between the life bound down to the negative shadowland of regulations and the positive persuasiveness of a totally new quality of existence made known in Christ. Thus he begins with the glorious affirmation, "If ye then be risen with Christ" (Col. 3:1).

"Christ," said Paul, "has lifted you up." You could never have lifted yourself up. You have been talking about a death through self-discipline and abasement. This is the death that ends in death. You can never lift yourself up by dying. To die is to go down into the pit of gloom to be no more. Only by dying with Christ, by identifying yourself with his death, by dying to the things which made his death necessary can you be raised to live in heavenly places with Christ.

When this happens, mortality is here and now swallowed up by life. This is not a mild reformation of one's outward conduct. It is the regeneration of life, a transformation from the realm of death to the realm of life. This is the miracle of the new birth. And it is a miracle; it is not simply a gradual metamorphosis of character.

So often we make religion the product of a gradual process of inevitable progress. This is not the New Testament picture. There is a kind of progressive revelation in history, but it is not the product of the historical process. G. Preston MacLeod speaks most convincingly of this:

> One might expect that the most inspired expressions of Christian truth, and the most creative moments of Christian witness, would come only when the human environment was most favorable. This is sometimes true, as when the Holy Spirit descended on a prepared and expectant company at Pentecost, though it must not be forgotten that the wider context of their meeting was a world that had just crucified Christ. . . . Basically, however, the gospel is not the crown and flower of a wholesome civilization that moves inevitably toward it. The gospel is God's invasion of a sinful and lost world. The strongest kind of evidence of the power and love of God in this world is found in the events of history which show how God, working through devoted Christians, has released into the most unpromising

and discreditable human situations creative influences for good. . . . The divine love shines forth most gloriously from the Cross. And when the human situation is most unfavorable, those who count as the mightiest factor in their environment the influence of Jesus Christ can turn a negative situation into an occasion of great good for the world.[1]

He demonstrates his thesis by three of the best known and best loved passages of Scripture which followed in fast succession in 1 Corinthians. You might expect to find these passages written to a church which had inspired the writer by their unity and love. Exactly the opposite was true. The earliest recording of the Lord's Supper (1 Cor. 11:23-26), an account "which has hallowed that sacred feast throughout all Christendom," was prompted by the unseemly, snobbish, and degrading misuse of the Communion in the Christian church.

The most sublime hymn to love ever written came out of "a discreditable and love-destroying dispute born of human pride as to who could claim the highest spiritual attainments." Again the greatest affirmation on the life everlasting which has lifted the hopes of the bereaved into eternity in every Christian generation (1 Cor. 15) was born out of a barren intellectual dispute over human theories of the life after death.

These deathless affirmations of the deathless life in Christ are not philosophical conclusions based on the brightness of our earthly existence but on the bright dawn that suddenly broke upon the world on the resurrection morning. The hope blazed out of the belief that he who walked the dark trail to triumph would one day tread the clouds of glory.

There is nothing we can do to raise ourselves into newness of life. This has been done for us—"If ye then be risen with Christ." But there is something which we must do as a consequence. If a man is risen with Christ it must follow as the night the day that he must seek the things above, where "Christ sitteth on the right hand of God," where Christ is in control. We must focus our desires and thoughts on heaven, the realm where our risen Master reigns.

We do not seek the things which are above in order that we may win heaven but because Christ has translated us into a new level of life and these are the things that belong to the new world. By our Christian confession of faith and baptism we said farewell to the old life in the realm of shadows. Thus we moved into a higher country of shining light, a country where truth and purity and honor and love are the way of life.

Paul said, "Set your affection on things above, not on things on the earth" (Col. 3:2). The imperative is in the present tense which describes a continuing attitude. The set of the Christian's mind is on the eternal. There is a Christian otherworldliness, and we should not be ashamed of it. Unfortunately, this otherworldliness is often interpreted as a flight from the grim, hard realities of life, a refusal to stand up to our immediate responsibilities, to work for the improvement of this world. In truth, those who have contributed most to the lifting of this world have placed their fulcrum and lever and taken their stand in the "city which hath foundations, whose builder and maker is God" (Heb. 11:10).

This must be so, for the Christian's life is hid with Christ in God. It is hid in the sense that it is shrouded in mystery. No rational explanation can be given as to how a man can live in Christ and share his cleansing, redeeming power. It is hid also in the sense that it is perfectly serene. Spiritual corrosion can never set in, for Christ has wrapped him around with his own eternity.

It is hid also in the sense that its essential glory has not yet been revealed. The unveiling of the Christian glory will be manifested when Christ comes in glorious majesty to end this earthly order. The essence of the Christian's life is in Christ. When Christ's glory is fully revealed, then the glory of the Christian life will be unfolded.

Thus wrote John, "It doth not yet appear what we shall be: but we know that, when he shall appear, we shall be like him; for we shall see him as he is" (1 John 3:2).

Notes

1. Beare and MacLeod, *op. cit.*, pp. 209-10.

22. Foundations for Morality

Colossians 3:1-5

Paul's interpretation of Christianity moves entirely around the union of the believer with Christ. This union takes place at conversion when the believer dies with Christ and is raised with Christ. All of Paul's theology is an interpretation of this death to sin and resurrection to walk in newness of life. This is the meaning of Christian baptism. It symbolizes this radical transition from death to life. In verses 1-4 of chapter 3, Paul makes this the link between his theological and his ethical position. He sees no other foundation upon which to build a Christian ethic which enables us to enter into his death and resurrection than this mystical union with the Redeemer.

The aorist tense of the verb should be given full force, "you died with Christ. You have been raised with Christ. You must, therefore, let the steady drift of your life be in the direction of Christ." Between the believer and Jesus Christ there is a union so close that the destiny of the believer can be read in the destiny of Christ. In the second coming the Christian's glory will be manifested at the same time with the manifestation of Christ's glory.

Yet, even now the Christian's life must be noticeably different. During the Crimean War Florence Nightingale was the angel of the troops. One day as she passed through the ward a soldier looked up from his cot of agony and cried, "You are Christ to me." Then he died. Is this not what Paul meant when he wrote, "Ye are our epistle written in our hearts, known and read of all men" (2 Cor. 3:2).

When, after all his sinfulness, Jacob turned homeward, he looked forward with grave anxiety to meeting the brother he had wronged. When big-hearted Esau received him back, Jacob said, "I have seen thy face, as though I had seen the face of God" (Gen. 33:10). The forgiveness of Esau made the forgiveness of God believable.

A great German mystic was on trial before the German court. After hearing his testimony, one arose and said, "You had better let that man go. Who knows what is behind that life?" The court saw that his life was connected with some supernatural power.

Although Paul says that the Christian life is hid in Christ, it is also on constant display. Here mysticism on its highest level and eschatology on its highest level meet. The Christian glory is not yet fully revealed, but it is none the less real in history. The body of glory is laid up in heaven, but the conduct of a Christian reflects the glory of Christ on earth. Here Paul unites not only mysticism and eschatology but also ties his ethics indissolubly into these. For Paul, mysticism, eschatology, and ethics belong together. By the mystical union of the believer with his Lord, he shares not only the hope of the life eternal but also eternal life itself. Christ is not simply the giver of that life. He is the life. Jesus did not simply say, "Here is life eternal." He said, "I am it!" God does not simply give us a life like his; rather does he give us the very life of God himself. When God created us, we were somewhat different from God. But when God begets us in the birth which is from above, we get the *zōē,* the life of God. Jesus said, "He that hath the Son hath life" (1 John 5:12). Paul wrote that we shall be "fashioned like unto his glorious body" (Phil. 3:21).

In essence, the Christian ethic is a description of a life which in Christ triumphs over all things temporal, which are destined to pass away.

The Christian acknowledges himself as a pilgrim in a foreign land. His homeland is above in a better world. When a true man is away from home, his thoughts are always turning homeward. He dreams about home. He writes letters to his dear ones. He may not be faraway, but he will never be at rest until he is back at home. The Christian's true life centers in the city of God. Here there is no abiding city.

This is no cowardly negativism. It is the solid spiritual truth that the optimistic view of history itself is false. There is no proof in history that all things are coming out Christ's way. Think of those great churches of the past—the seven churches of Asia Minor all lie in ruin now. There is in history no proof of the cosmic claims of Christ. The only proof is in the resurrection of Jesus. This we can know, not through scientific proof, but through faith.

The coming of Christ's kingdom will not be in history but above history. It will be the shattering of history when the heavenly Jerusalem comes down. Christ's parable of the seed means that goodness does not win the day on earth. The tares remain until the end. Yet this is not to lead the Christian toward an indifferent withdrawal from the task of making this world a better place. The Christian knows that all things good will survive in God's higher kingdom. His efforts and achievements will not always be frustrated. In God's higher kingdom nothing good will be finally lost.

Paul, therefore, would never recognize a Christian mysticism nor a Christian eschatology which did not produce a Christian ethic. Paul had no systematic ethic. His was the ethic of the Spirit seen in Romans 8:13: "For if ye live after the flesh, ye shall die: but if . . . through the Spirit . . . ye shall live."

Paul then passes from the theological foundations to declare his ethic of death and resurrection with Christ. Said he, "Put to death therefore what is earthly in you" (Col. 3:5, RSV). On the surface there seems to be a contradiction here. Paul has said, "Ye died." Now he says, "You must put to death." He is simply saying: "You must actualize your ideal death in Christ. This must be done every day. You must put the new principle of your life into action." In his Roman letter (6:8-11, RSV), Paul wrote, "We have died with Christ. . . . So you also must consider yourselves dead to sin and alive to God in Christ Jesus." Become what in fact you are.

Here arises the old debate between those who say salvation is of God, what then is there for us to do? Paul never divorced the divine action from the human response. God redeems by enabling men to respond and to work out the salvation which God is giving.

In 1 John, we read in one place, "Whosoever is born of God doth not commit sin" (1 John 3:9). And in another we read, "If we say that we have no sin, we deceive ourselves" (1 John 1:8). The writer meant that in principle the Christian life does not make a practice of sin but in actuality, during mortal life, it never fully triumphs over sin.

Every day we must die to sin. Objectively, God's victory is already won. The atonement has been completed. Satan has fallen as lightning from heaven. Yet the fight goes on until the last trumpet.

23. The Garments of the Ungodly

Colossians 3:5-9

In almost every university I know it has become fashionable for a few professors to spend a good deal of time seeking to persuade young people that there are no moral absolutes in our world. Our moral standards, they say, are but the results of the mores of our forebears. Usually they are the archaic carry-over of the Medieval age and should have no place in our enlightened days.

Believing this, they say to our students: "Your life is your own. It is the only life you will ever have. No one must be allowed to tell you what you must do with it. You must, above all else, be free to make your own rules, even if it means the flaunting of all the rules of the past!"

Now, that sounds marvelously appealing, especially when the heart is light and the rich, red blood is dancing madly in the veins. "Why," we ask, "should I be shackled by shibboleths mumbled over me by my parents, mumbled over them by their parents? To the rubbish heap of history with all such unpleasant fetters!"

Of course, no professor that I know wants to be responsible for the unpleasant consequences of irresponsible living and disregard for the laws of life which are as old as the race. He leaves the unpleasant aftermath of heartbreak and ruin in the hands of pastors and counselors.

This is the reason a Christian pastor must say: "You cannot take life into your own hands. Life is God's gift to you. You must begin with God. You are here because God put you here, and there is no other reason for your being here."

God is the author of certain moral absolutes; and if you violate them, life becomes unbearable. The concomitant of believing that you are absolutely free is the denial of the existence of a God who cares about you. If there is no God, then you must be your own god and then you can be absolutely free. Yet, when you choose to follow your own whims, you come into certain consequences which show you that there is a moral law which takes its toll in the conscience. Behind this moral law is a moral God. The soul in such anarchy cries out for moral absolutes and for a God who has the right to tell us what is right for us.

If men can ignore God, they can ignore all lesser authority. They can ignore their parents, their pastors, their judges who sit on benches of authority. The result of absolute freedom is absolute anarchy.

Here is the young person who says: "Speed limits were made for those old crocks whose arthritic joints won't permit them to stop rapidly. I'm young. I'm the master of this machine. I'll make my own speed limits." So he wraps his father's station wagon around a telephone pole, snuffs out his own life, shatters his parent's dreams, shakes their nervous systems until they walk through life ever after in a fog. He injures another who must lie in his bed of agony month after month while his family goes hopelessly in debt to pay medical bills. All this he does in the name of freedom.

Young people, remember, you may be free to flaunt your defiance in the face of the moral laws of God, but you are not free to repair the damage of such defiance.

We are in an undisciplined world. Sören Kierkegaard created a theology of the disordered world which has found a name in existentialism. Some years ago, I visited the hangouts of the existentialists on the left bank of the Seine in Paris. These weird fathers of the American beatniks were there. There you find total pessimism toward any of the ordered processes of life—girls with their hair pasted flat, wearing cat-eye make-up, ill-fitting sweaters and tight trousers. There were men with wild beards living in absolute defiance of that self-discipline which is the result of our belief in a divine creation.

Now, the apostle Paul insists that the Christian life is a disciplined life and that the only true freedom is the result of discipline. He did not oppose asceticism because it was too harsh on the flesh but because it was not harsh enough. It did not suppress and control sensuality. Paul said that it is not enough to regulate the life of the flesh, we must eradicate it.

"Put to death," he says, "what is earthly in you" (Col. 3:5, RSV). Then after the popular fashion of the time, he lists a pentad of vices.

First, immorality and impurity must be put to death. The pagan world regarded the sexual appetite not as something to be suppressed but as something to be gratified and given free reign. Chastity was an utterly new virtue which Christianity introduced into the pagan world. Paul saw that the true function of sex could be fulfilled only in purity as the bonds of marriage vows were kept strong and secure by absolute faithfulness to the marriage vows. The only love that endures is that in which one man loves one woman so much that he does not care to love another in the same way.

Passion and evil desire must die. A Christian cannot be a slave to his passions. He must not be driven by desire for that which is wrong.

Coveteousness must go down in death. This word *pleonexia* is a combination of two Greek words. *Pleon* means more and *echein* means to have. Combined they mean the desire to have more. It is the opposite of the desire to give. More explicitly, it is man's hunger for that to which he has no right. It is a sin which is equated with idolatry, for a man's god is that which he desires most and loves most. If he covets money, coveteousness may lead him to dishonesty and to making mammon his god. If he covets position, coveteousness may lead him to ruthless disregard of others and prestige may become his god. If he covets his neighbor's wife, he may even murder and sensual pleasure may become his god.

Idolatry is an attempt to use God for man's purposes rather than to give one's self to God's service. This is the reason the wrath of God falls on the sons of disobedience. God's wrath is not a divine temper tantrum. It is the implacable, unbending opposition of God to man's sin. Someone has said, "I could not love a father who did not love me enough to be angry with me when I do wrong and I could not worship a God who did not love me enough to be angry with the sin which destroys the best within me." "He that soweth to his flesh shall of the flesh reap corruption" (Gal. 6:8).

Then Paul comes to call us to "put off the garments of ungodliness." He has called us to kill the sins of the appetite. Now he calls us to put off, as a garment, the sins of the temper and the tongue.

Isaiah said, "He hath clothed me with the garments of salvation, he hath covered me with the robe of righteousness, as a bridegroom decketh himself with ornaments, and as a bride adorneth herself with her jewels" (Isa. 61:10).

John wrote, "Blessed is he that watcheth, and keepeth his garments" (Rev. 16:15). "He that overcometh, the same shall be clothed in white raiment" (Rev. 3:5). "After this I beheld, and, lo, a great multitude, which no man could number, of all nations, and kindreds, and people, and tongues, stood before the throne, and before the Lamb, clothed with white robes, and palms in their hands" (Rev. 7:9).

Again Isaiah said, "All our righteousnesses are as filthy rags" (Isa. 64:6).

In the early days, when a Christian was baptized, when he went down into the waters, he put off his old clothes and when he emerged he was clothed in a new robe, pure and white. Thus, he symbolized his laying aside the old conduct and his taking on a new kind of life.

Paul calls every Christian to put off the garments of ungodliness composed of: temper—that sudden flame of fury which would devour as fire raging in straw; wrath—the settled, smoldering hostility which refuses to be placated; malice—the desire to harm others; slander—reviling one's fellow men; foul talk—from your mouth may mean obscene language or loud abuse which utterly crushes another. How much damage can be done to the reputation and spirit of a man by the uncontrolled tongue!

Paul then adds a particular injunction against lying. "This," says he, "belongs to the old nature." A man in Christ is a man of truth. Paul insists that if a man clings to these things as the pattern of his life there is no evidence that his nature has been changed.

"You must," says he, "be men who have put off the old deeds." The word for "put off" is translated in Colossians 2:15 (RSV), as "disarmed." It sounds the note of triumph over the evil habits which belonged to the old life. Are there habits which belie your Christian profession—unclean speech, impurity, untruthfulness? Do you delight to slander others?

Then, said Paul, "You must make your calling and election sure by renouncing these. Put on the garments of God's grace as you join those who have washed their garments and made them white in the blood of the Lamb."

24. Universal Redemption

Colossians 3:9b-14

Christian conversion brings a change so complete that Paul could liken it to the stripping off of an old garment which was to be finally discarded and the putting on of a pure, fresh garment. The glory of the Christian life is that it is continually being renewed. It never grows old. It cannot be corrupted by time. Every moment it is taking upon itself more of the image of the Creator. God is ever clothing his own with fresh garments. In Genesis 3:21, we read, "Unto Adam also and to his wife did the Lord God make coats of skins, and clothed them." In 2 Chronicles 6:41 is the admonition, "Let thy priests . . . be clothed with salvation." The psalmist said, "Thou art clothed with honour and majesty" (Psalm 104:1).

So Paul uses an ancient metaphor when he says, "Put on the new self which is ever freshly renewed until it reaches fulness of knowledge in the likeness of its Creator."

The translation should be not "in knowledge" but "unto knowledge." The meaning is that as we grow in the likeness of God, as his holiness, beauty, and glory come to be our own, we have a vital knowledge of God which no one can share outside this experience.

In this new life all social and cultural distinctions go down and the original unity of the race is restored. Immorality, covetousness, anger, malice, slander, and falsehood divide humanity into hostile camps. As a result, one nation hates another, one race hates another, and even the advocates of one religion can hate the advocates of another.

In Christ all such hatred must go down. In him there cannot be the Greek, the proud aristocrat, and the scholar putting the love of philosophy above the love of people; there cannot be the proud Jew, feeling that he alone is the chosen of the Lord and that all others were ordained to provide fuel for the fires of hell.

There cannot be circumcized and uncircumcized. These outward symbols mean nothing apart from the circumcision of the heart made possible by God's redeeming grace which works the miracle of regeneration. There cannot be the barbaric Persians and Egyptians, the cultivated Orientals, nor the rude savage Scythians from the northern wilds. All of these are redeemed and united.

In the kingdom of redemption Christ is all and in all. This means that when men are in Christ, this relationship transcends all racial, national, and cultural ties and destroys all barriers which separate man from his brother.

In Christ all men share the prerogatives which once belonged to Israel. They are a new people with three characteristics: they are chosen, holy, and beloved. Because this is true of them, they are to put on the garments which betoken their new status. In his Galatian letter, Paul wrote, "As many of you as have been baptized into Christ have put on Christ" (Gal. 3:27). The garments of grace include:

Compassion.—The ancient world was hard and cruel before Christ came. The poor were pushed to the wall. There was no care for the aged, the infirm, or the mentally ill until Christ breathed his compassion upon his followers.

Kindness.—This is the quality which considers our neighbor's welfare as important as our own. Josephus used this word to describe Isaac who dug wells and gave them to others because he refused to fight over them. This word also was used to describe wine which was mellow with age and whose harshness had vanished. A moral man outside of Christ is often stern and forbidding. Only in Christ is goodness and kindness combined. Jesus was kind to the lowest of sinners, for he was the Son of a Father who "sendeth rain on the just and on the unjust" (Matt. 5:45).

Humility.—This was a virtue introduced by Christ. Not in the sense that it was not known before, for Micah had listed it among the irreducible requirements of God. "What doth the Lord require of thee, but to do justly, and to love mercy, and to walk humbly with thy God" (Mic. 6:8). This virtue had fallen into disrepute. In classical Greek there is no word for humility which does not denote a groveling servility. Christ lifted humility above this degrading self-abasement by basing it upon two things: the honest acknowledgement of the fact that we are creatures and that God is the Creator and the recognition that all men belong to the royal family of God. An attitude of arrogance and condescension toward another is utterly out of place.

Gentleness.—William Barclay, who has a splendid treatment of this entire passage and from whom I have drawn much, writes:

> Long ago Aristotle had defined *praotes* [gentleness]as the happy mean between too much and too little anger. The man who has *praotes* is the man who is so self-controlled, because he is God-controlled, that he is always angry at the right time and never angry at the wrong time. He has at one and the same time the strength and the sweetness of true gentleness.[1]

Patience.—Embodied here is the attitude which forbears with all the stubborn stupidity of men and refuses to give way to cynical despair. The enduring longsuffering with those who slander and abuse us is patience.

Forbearance and forgiveness.—Here the Christian's forgiveness is not based on a divine command nor upon the example of Christ but upon the personal experience of forgiveness. "God for Christ's sake hath forgiven you" (Eph. 4:32). As you are a forgiven man, so must you be forgiving toward others.

Roy A. Burkhart tells of a boy who went out of his home to do something that his parents felt was wrong. He was involved in an accident and lost both legs.

It was a terrible blow, but the father told me one of the most beautiful stories I have ever heard. He said, "When his mother and I saw him in the hospital cot lying there aware that he had lost both legs, he said, 'Will you forgive me?' " They both ran up, hugged him and said, "Of course, we have already forgiven you." And he answered, "Then, I can live without my legs."[2]

Irving Stone, in *Love Is Eternal,* concludes his narrative account of Mary Todd and Abraham Lincoln with an interview between Mrs. Lincoln and Parker, the President's guard:

Parker entered, a heavy-faced man with half-closed lids. He trembled.

"Why were you not at the door to keep the assassin out?" she asked fiercely.

Parker hung his head.

"I have bitterly repented it. But I did not believe that anyone would try to kill so good a man in such a public place. The belief made me careless. I was attracted by the play, and did not see the assassin enter the box."

"You should have seen him. You had no business to be careless." She fell back on the pillow, covered her face with her hands. "Go now. It's not you I can't forgive, it's the assassin."

"If Pa had lived," said Tad, "he would have forgiven the man who shot him. Pa forgave everybody."[3]

J. B. Lightfoot reminds us that one of the greatest tributes paid to Christianity was paid not by a theologian but by a master linguist.

Max Müller was one of the great experts of the science of language. Now, in the ancient world, no one was interested in foreign languages, apart from Greek. There was no learning and no studying of foreign languages. The Greeks were the scholars, and they would never have deigned to study a barbarian tongue. The science of language is a new science, and the desire to know other languages a new desire. And Max Müller wrote: "Not till that word *barbarian* was struck out of the dictionary of mankind, and replaced by *brother,* not till the right of all nations of the world to be classed as members of one genus or kind was recognized, can we look even for the first beginnings of our science of language. . . . This change was effected by Christianity." It was Christianity which drew men together sufficiently [to cause them] to wish to know each other's languages.[4]

The bond that binds all the virtues together is love. Love provides the ligaments that hold the body of Christ together, for the function of love is to bind Christians together. When these virtues are bound together in each Christian and all Christians are bound together in love, there is the perfecting of which the Master spoke when he said, "Be ye therefore perfect, even as your Father which is in heaven is perfect" (Matt. 5:48).

"Let the harmony of God reign in your hearts, remembering that as members of the same body you are called to live in harmony, and never forget to be thankful for what God has done for you" (Col. 3:15, Phillips). Paul took a word from the athletic arena which was used when the umpire settled a dispute. When there is a clash between Christians, the peace of God must be the decider. That course of action must be taken which will not break the peace of the Christian body, the church.

Notes

1. Barclay, *op. cit.,* p. 189.
2. Quoted in Wallis, *Speakers' Illustrations for Special Days,* pp. 94-95.
3. Irving Stone, *Love Is Eternal* (New York: Doubleday & Co., Inc., 1954), p. 133. By permission.
4. Barclay, *op. cit.,* p. 186.

25. The Indwelling Word of Christ

Colossians 3:16

Let us think together of how our worship may be made more vital, inspiring, and uplifting. Worship is the most important work the children of God do in this world. William Temple, in a broadcast to the United States, said:

I am disposed to begin by making what many people will feel to be a quite outrageous statement. This world can be saved from political chaos and collapse by one thing only, and that is worship. For to worship is to quicken the conscience by the holiness of God, to feed the mind with truth of God, to purge the imagination by the beauty of God, to open up the heart to the love of God, to devote the will to the purpose of God.[1]

Think of the apostle Paul's concept of church music. He wrote to the Colossian congregation, "Let the word of Christ dwell in you richly, as you teach and admonish one another in all wisdom, and as you sing psalms and hymns and spiritual songs with thankfulness in your hearts to God" (Col. 3:16, RSV).

Great music has always been a part of great religion. Pliny, the Roman governor of Bithynia, once wrote a letter to the Emperor

Trajan to describe a Christian community he had found. The most distinctive thing he could say about the people was, "They meet at dawn to sing a song of praise unto Christ as unto God."

The Christian faith was born in song. Creation's bright morning was filled with song. Said Job, "The morning stars sang together, and all the sons of God shouted for joy" (Job 38:7).

When God began his new creation with the advent of Christ, the heavens were filled with angel voices singing, "Glory to God in the highest" (Luke 2:14).

The Christian martyrs sang until their shriveled lips could form the words no more.

In the days of Moody's great revivals, men often heard the great revivalist unmoved until Sankey stood up to sing, "There Were Ninety and Nine." Then all the defenses of the hardest man went down.

Paul knew that music in the church must be different from all other music; otherwise it would grow dull, morose, and repelling. Therefore, he said that all true spiritual music must be the spontaneous overflow of the heart in which Christ dwells.

"Let the word of Christ dwell in you richly." Not in scant measure and not as a temporary guest, but let the living Christ make his settled, permanent abode in the rich fulness of his grace and power in your heart.

"The word of Christ" means Christ himself, who is the monitor of the redeemed soul. From him comes permanent inspiration and guidance. This is the fulfilment of Jeremiah's prophecy of the new covenant. This is the essence of the New Testament. "After those days, saith the Lord, I will put my law in their inward parts, and write it in their hearts; and will be their God, and they shall be my people" (Jer. 31:33).

The rich indwelling of Christ assures us that our hearts will overflow in melody to the Lord. If worship and singing are dull, it is because Jesus Christ does not dwell in the heart.

In the popular mind in Paul's day the word, or the "logos," symbolized the divine essence, the rational principle, imminent in the universe and present in every soul. For Paul the logos was not a vague, abstract, philosophical idea but a personal presence. Christ himself was the "logos," even as John had written. "The Word [Logos] was made flesh, and dwelt among us, . . . full of grace and truth" (John 1:14).

When Christ dwells in the heart, men are inspired to share him with others. This they do, as Paul said, by "teaching and admonishing one another in all wisdom." One of the greatest instruments for teaching the doctrines of our faith is our church music.

Oscar Hammerstein II, who died a short time ago, wrote those warm and winsome words about beautiful mornings and enchanted evenings. In reporting his death a commentator told of his saying once, "A song writer wants above all else to hear his songs sung by as many people as possible, as long as possible."

So often we are moved to think of music as having to do solely with the inspirational side of worship and I do believe this is its major function. Yet the examples of early Christian hymnody in the New Testament were full of solid, substantial Christian truth.

It is strongly believed that this sublime confession of Christian truth and faith found in 1 Timothy 3:16, is a part of an early Christian hymn:

Great is the mystery of godliness:
God was manifest in the flesh,
Justified in the Spirit,
Seen of angels,
Preached unto the Gentiles,
Believed on in the world,
Received up into glory.

Many of our great hymns are comprehensive statements of Christian truth. Christian worship soars to its most sublime height of inspiration and to its loftiest level of Christian instruction when we sing:

Fairest, Lord Jesus, Ruler of all nature,
O Thou of God and man the Son;
Thee will I cherish, Thee will I honor,
Thou, my soul's glory, joy, and crown.

Fair are the meadows, Fairer still the woodlands,
Robed in the blooming garb of spring;
Jesus is fairer, Jesus is purer,
Who makes the woeful heart to sing.

Fair is the sunshine, Fairer still the moonlight
And all the twinkling, starry host;
Jesus shines brighter, Jesus shines purer
Than all the angels heaven can boast.

The Christian hymnal is filled with the highest expressions of Christian doctrine ever to flow through the heart of man touched by the Spirit of God. The Christian church has literally sung her way across the centuries. The oldest hymn in the Christian hymnal bears the hauntingly beautiful title, "Shepherd of Tender Youth." It was written by Clement of Alexandria, who for many years was head of the first-known Christian school, the Catechetical school of Alexandria which dates back to about A.D. 200. It was translated by H. M. Dexter in 1846:

Shepherd of tender youth,
Guiding in love and truth,
Through devious ways;
Christ our triumphant King,
We come Thy name to sing,
Hither our children bring
To shout Thy praise.

Methodist hymnody became the most powerful evangelizing influence in England. "Jesus, Thy Boundless Love to Me" was written in the seventeenth century by Paul Gerhardt and translated in the eighteenth century by John Wesley. It was set to music by Henri F. Hemy in the nineteenth century.

Jesus, Thy boundless love to me
  No tho't can reach, no tongue declare;
Oh, knit my thankful heart to Thee
  And reign without a rival there:
Thine wholly, Thine alone, I am;
  Be Thou alone my constant flame.

O love, how gracious is Thy way!
  All fear before Thy presence flies:
Care, anguish, sorrow melt away,
  Where'er Thy healing beams arise:
O Jesus, nothing may I see,
  Nothing desire, or seek, but Thee;

In suff'ring, be Thy love my peace;
  In weakness, be Thy love my pow'r;
And when the storms of life shall cease,
  Jesus, in that eventful hour,
In death, as life, be Guide and Friend,
  That I may love Thee without end.

Paul commanded that we are also to admonish one another in psalms and hymns and spiritual songs. Christ who is the inner voice, who is constantly counseling and guiding his own, has implanted his message so deeply in the believer's heart that it permeates all his thinking. Paul did not think of religion so much as an interest in itself but as the living power behind all other interests. Therefore, all the wealth of the wisdom of the Christian gospel dwells in the believer to enable him to teach and admonish others.

Since it is of Christ that every Christian seeks to bear witness, it is of him we should sing. Christian hymns should center around his birth, his life, his teachings, his death, resurrection, ascension, and triumphant return. One whose heart is wholly given to him can never tire of singing:

I've found a friend, oh, such a friend!
  He loved me ere I knew Him;
He drew me with the cords of love,
  And thus He bound me to Him;
And round my heart still closely twine
Those ties which naught can sever,
For I am His, and He is mine,
  Forever and forever.

JAMES G. SMALL

For sheer transporting rapture here is a theme to lift the forlorn heart:

O Love of God most full,
O Love of God most free,
Come, warm my heart,
Come, fill my soul,
Come, lead me unto Thee!

The wildest sea is calm,
The tempest brings no fear,
The darkest night
Is full of light
Because Thy love is near.

OSCAR CLUTE

Notes

1. Quoted in Kennedy, *op. cit.*, pp. 350-51.

26. A Singing Religion

*Colossians 3:16*b

On the Plymouth Rock monument is a challenge every American should heed:

> This spot marks the final resting place of the Pilgrims of the Mayflower. In weariness and hunger and in cold, fighting the wilderness and burying their dead in common graves that the Indians should not know how many had perished, they here laid the foundations of a state in which all men for countless ages should have liberty to worship God in their own way. All you who pass . . . dedicate yourselves anew to the resolution that you will not rest until this lofty ideal shall have been realized throughout the earth.[1]

Many have interpreted freedom of worship to mean freedom from worship. To refrain from worship is to enslave one's self to the temporal. To worship is to be in touch with the eternal.

> For worship is a thirsty land crying out
> for rain,
> It is a candle in the act of being kindled,
> It is a drop in quest of the ocean, . . .
> It is a voice in the night calling for help,
> It is a soul standing in awe before the
> mystery of the universe, . . .
> It is time flowing into eternity, . . .
> A man climbing the altar stairs to God.[2]

One of the loftiest aids to worship which God has given us is music. Years ago a writer, whose name has been lost, wrote this tribute to music:

Servant and Master am I; servant of those dead and master of those living. Through me spirits immortal speak the message that makes the world weep, and laugh, and wonder, and worship. I tell the story of love, the story of hate, the story that saves, and the story that damns. I am the incense upon which prayers float to heaven. I am the smoke which palls over the field of battle where men lie dying with me on their lips. I am close to the marriage altar, and when the graves open I stand near by. I call the wanderer home, I rescue the soul from the depths, I open the lips of lovers, and through me the dead whisper to the living. One I serve as I serve all; and the king I make my slave as easily as I subject his slave. I speak through the birds of the air, the insects of the field, the crash of waters on rock-ribbed shores, the sighing of wind in the trees, and I am even heard by the soul that knows me in the clatter of wheels on city streets. I know no brother, yet all men are my brothers; I am the father of the best that is in them, and they are fathers of the best that is in me; I am of them, and they are of me. For I am the instrument of God.[3]

Music has always been one of God's most sublime instruments. Concerning singing, multiple commands are found in the Bible. Isaiah said, "Ye shall have a song, as in the night when a holy solemnity is kept; and gladness of heart, as when one goeth with a pipe to come into the mountain of the Lord, to the mighty One of Israel" (Isa. 30:29). James wrote, "Is any among you afflicted? let him pray. Is any merry? let him sing psalms" (James 5:13).

Music was recognized in the days of David as an instrument for the cure of souls. When Saul was sick, he sent not for a physician nor a soothsayer to chase away the madness, bitterness, and despair but for David, the sweet singer of Israel. "David took an harp, and played with his hand: so Saul was refreshed, and was well, and the evil spirit departed from him" (1 Sam. 16:23).

Israel was a singing people. All her sacred processions were accompanied by singing. This is the reason I am mightily stirred by processional singing. As the ark of the covenant was borne into Jerusalem on the greatest day of David's life, the choir sang, "Lift up your heads" (Psalm 24:7). The gates were not high enough for his Majesty. The choir challenges his entrance, "Who is this King of glory?" (v. 8). Then the mighty refrain rings out, "The Lord of hosts, he is the King of glory" (v. 10).

At all formal dedications "the trumpeters and singers were as one, to make one sound to be heard in praising and thanking the Lord" (2 Chron. 5:13). They sang their songs of harvest. At their great feasts they sang. Thus we read at the Lord's Supper, "when they had sung an hymn, they went out into the mount of Olives" (Matt. 26:30).

They sang after military victories. Note the song of Miriam after the Exodus: "Sing ye to the Lord, for he hath triumphed gloriously; the horse and his rider hath he thrown into the sea" (Ex. 15:21).

They sang at the close of life. We read in Ecclesiastes 12:4, "And the doors shall be shut in the streets, when the sound of the grinding is low, and he shall rise up at the voice of the bird, and all the daughters of musick shall be brought low."

And the innumerable choir shall sing the redeemed home to their rest. They shall lift up the magnificat of heaven, singing, "To the only wise God our Saviour, be glory and majesty, dominion and power, both now and ever. Amen" (Jude 25).

The birth of the Redeemer was accompanied by the song of the angels, "Glory to God in the highest" (Luke 2:14), and by the Magnificat of Mary, the virgin mother:

> My soul doth magnify the Lord,
> And my spirit hath rejoiced in God my Saviour.
> For he hath regarded the low estate of his handmaiden:
> For, behold, from henceforth all generations shall call me blessed.

For he that is mighty hath done to me great things;
and holy is his name.
And his mercy is on them that fear him
from generation to generation.
He hath shewed strength with his arm;
He hath scattered the proud in the imagination of their hearts.
He hath put down the mighty from their seats,
and exalted them of low degree.
He hath filled the hungry with good things;
and the rich he hath sent empty away.
He hath holpen his servant Israel,
in remembrance of his mercy;
As he spake to our fathers,
to Abraham, and to his seed for ever (Luke 1:46-55).

Our Lord's return will be marked by music. Our Lord's return in glorious majesty will be accompanied by a "shout, with the voice of the archangel, and with the trump of God: and the dead in Christ shall rise first" (1 Thess. 4:16).

Music plays so vital a role in the worship and work of God that the Bible teaches that singers must be appointed. In a sense, they are ordained to serve God through music. Second Chronicles 20:21 reads: "And when he had consulted with the people, he appointed singers unto the Lord."

No person should sing in a church choir who is not deeply committed to Christ and whose soul is not in his singing. No professionalism is in place there. The quarreling over contracts by paid "prima donnas," who will not sing on Sunday evening because they are not paid to is an abomination to the Lord.

Israel could not sing "the Lord's song in a strange land" (Psalm 137:4). Neither can any estranged soul sing to the glory of God. Music in the church loses its lilt and lifting power when professionalism intervenes. The great choirs of history have been composed of people wholly consecrated to Christ, who knew that only the best was worthy of use in the worship of the Lord of glory.

Great choirs are made by consecrated people who are willing to work. Flabby voices come from flabby souls. Solomon's great temple choir was not the result of an accidental collocation of heterogeneous musicians. It was the result of great toil. All great music has been wrung out of the anguish of men's souls and can never be sung at its best apart from the anguish and toil of those who sing it.

The choirmaster who is paid to provide heaven's music for a congregation is guilty of sacrilege if he does not labor tirelessly to find consecrated people with God-given voices to sing in the choir and if he does not inspire them to work tirelessly until flawless music, which heaven can honor, comes from the choir loft.

The greatest threat in the life of the modern church is a dispassionate professionalism on the part of a church staff. Any member of a church staff who does not do the work for which he is paid is worse than a thief, for he takes money which people have given for building the kingdom of God without making a contribution toward building that kingdom.

Every great revival of religion the world has ever known has been accompanied by great music. Paul said, "Let the word of Christ dwell in you richly in all wisdom; teaching and admonishing one another in psalms and hymns and spiritual songs, singing with grace in your hearts to the Lord" (Col. 3:16).

Examples of "psalms"—those regular poems modeled after the psalms of the Old Testament—may be found in the first chapter of Luke and in the book of Revelation. "Hymns" are those uplifting ascriptions of praise to Christ. "Spiritual songs" have been defined as those spontaneous outbursts of joy so like our southern Negro spirituals, the unpremeditated overflow of the soul upon which the spirit of God has moved.

Finally, Paul says, "singing with grace in your heart to the Lord." Grace here does not mean sweetness of melody nor excellence of musical merit. Paul was not thinking of poetic charm nor of the aesthetic quality of music. Paul is concerned supremely with the heartfelt devotion of the people to Christ. A heart in which Christ richly dwells is a heart that must at times burst forth in song. What music is ever more beautiful than that which sounds from a sincere soul, wholly given to God. No mocking pretense, no hypocritical flair or finesse; only the simple overflow of love for such singing is unto the Lord, not unto men.

During the war, on board a battleship, a friend of mine awoke to hear the purest Irish tenor he had ever heard coming from the lookout high above the waters. A boy, whom no one suspected as having any talent, was giving forth "The Lord's Prayer." This was truly music from the soul, no cheap substitute.

Those who were there tell that the most moving part of the Baptist World Alliance in Rio was the three thousand-voice choir. On the front row an eight-year-old Negro boy sang soprano. Beside him stood a seven-year-old white girl. They shared the same hymnal but scarcely looked at it. They sang music such as the "Hallelujah Chorus." There had been constant rehearsal. But more than that, every single night for three months a prayer meeting was held in every church, praying that Brazilian Baptists might measure up to their responsibility.

Paul summarizes his appeal with these words, "Whatsoever ye do in word or deed, do all in the name of the Lord Jesus" (Col. 3:17). The question every choirmaster and choir member should raise before standing before a worshiping congregation is, can I call upon the Lord Jesus to bless this music, asking him to be near and to move through it? Can I offer this to the hungry souls of men in the Saviour's name?

Notes

1. Quoted in Wallis, *A Treasury of Sermon Illustrations,* p. 292.
2. Dwight Bradley, quoted in *ibid.*
3. *Ibid.,* p. 214.

27. Specific Christian Duties

Colossians 3:18 to 4:1

The form of this passage is derived from the moral philosophy in vogue in the Hellenistic world. "There were philosophers who held that the function of philosophy was not to reveal the mysteries of the universe, but to advise mankind as to their conduct in the relations of domestic life. Paul himself may have felt no little sympathy with this point of view."[1]

Seneca said: "Some have allowed only that part of philosophy which tells the husband how to behave toward his wife, the father how to bring up his children, the master how to govern his slaves."

Here Paul gives counsel to the Christian husband, the Christian father, and the Christian master. Underlying the Pauline ethic is a deep reverence for a person as a person. "There is neither male nor female: for ye are all one in Christ Jesus" (Gal. 3:28).

Duties of Husbands and Wives

In the Greco-Roman world women were regarded as either toys or nuisances or, as under the Jewish law, they were regarded as chattel. A Jewish man owned his wife just as he owned his house. No Jewish woman could initiate divorce proceedings, for she had no legal rights.

It was the custom of the Greeks to confine their women to their apartments where they could not even join their menfolk for meals. Men could have as many sexual relationships outside of marriage as they desired without being censured while complete chastity was demanded of the women. It was a man's world in which men had all the privileges. It remained for Christianity to introduce into the world an ethic which placed mutual responsibilities upon men and women.

The ancient world, before Christ came, did not honor women. In the twenty-ninth year of Caesar, the very year of Christ's birth, a man who had gone away from his wife in Alexandria, wrote her a letter that said, "If the baby is a boy, keep it; if it is a girl, expose it."

In the new freedom which Christ had given his own, wives were still to be submissive to their husbands, but it was to be the submission of love, not of duty. The husbands were to show loving-kindness to their wives. The home which exists simply for the comfort and convenience of the husband and where the wife is regarded simply as a vessel to gratify her husband's desires cannot be a Christian home. The Christian home is founded "in Christ." In him there can be no harsh exploitation.

Duties of Parents and Children

Children, in the time of Paul, were under the control of their parents. The Roman *Patria Potestae,* the law of the father's power, gave him complete authority over the child. He had the power to sell him into slavery or even to sentence him to death and perform the execution. Paul recognized the obligation of the child to obey his parents; yet he also stressed the responsibility of the parent, which was not simply to discipline the child but also to encourage him. So often a parent is such a stern disciplinarian that he dismays the child and fills him with timidity and discouragement.

The obligation which Paul lays down is for children to obey Christian parents in all things. The phrase "in Christ" gives the assurance that these parents will not require of their children that which is wrong. It is said that Martin Luther's father was so stern that Luther found it exceedingly difficult to pray "Our Father." To him the word "father" symbolized forbidding severity. Luther, therefore, wrote, "Spare the rod and spoil the child. It is true; but beside the rod keep an apple to give him when he does well." Justice includes reward as well as punishment.

William Barclay relates:

> Sir Arnold Lunn, in *Memory to Memory,* quotes an incident about Field-Marshal Montgomery from a book by M. E. Clifton James. Montgomery was famous as a disciplinarian—but there was another side to him. Mr. Clifton James was Montgomery's official "double." He was studying Montgomery during a rehearsal for D-Day. "Within a few yards of where I was standing, a very young soldier, still looking sea-sick from his voyage, came struggling along gamely trying to keep up with his comrades in front. I could imagine that, feeling as he did, his rifle and equipment must have been like a ton weight. His heavy boots dragged in the sand, but I could see that he was fighting hard to conceal his distress. Just when he got level with us he tripped up, and fell flat on his face. Half sobbing, he heaved himself up and began to march off dazedly in the wrong direction. Monty went straight up to him and with a quick, friendly smile turned him around. "This way, sonny. You're doing well—very well. But don't lose touch with the chap in front of you." When the youngster realized who it was that had given him friendly help, his expression of dumb adoration was a study." It was just because Montgomery combined this discipline and encouragement that a private in the Eighth Army felt himself worth a colonel in any other army.
>
> The better a parent is the more he must avoid the danger of discouraging his child, for this parent must give discipline and encouragement in equal parts.[2]

Erethizete, which is translated provoked, could best be translated chafe. It denotes that irksome discipline which takes the heart out of children as they conclude that nothing they do can really please their parents.

Slaves and Masters

In verse 22, Paul addresses the slaves. Many feel that this passage is not firm enough. "Why," they ask, "did not Paul openly condemn the institution of slavery?" Possibly, he felt that slaves might mistake their freedom for the right to wage a social revolution. This would have engulfed the whole society in a devastating war which would have accomplished nothing. Possibly, Paul felt that the time had not yet come to raise the banner of social revolution. Paul, therefore, did not choose to fell the tree. He chose rather to ring the bark so that in time it would come down.

The ethics of the New Testament must be judged in the times written rather than in the times read. Paul's attitude was one of expediency. He knew that there are times when we must move slowly in order to move steadily.

Paul counsels the slaves to obey their master, remembering that their most menial service was a means of serving the Lord Christ. The Christian slave must not be continually asking, "What does my master owe me," but rather, "what do I owe him?" He must not simply work when the master's eye is upon him. He must recognize that he is working with his master and that both are serving the Lord Christ. Both slave and master have a common master—Jesus Christ—to whom they must finally give an account.

"Knowing that of the Lord ye shall receive the reward of the inheritance" (Col. 3:24). It cannot be fully appreciated how much this promise meant to a slave, for under Roman law he could possess nothing. Yet, here he is promised the very inheritance of God. At last, the scales of justice will be balanced. They who do God's work will get God's pay.

The employee who today lives only for a three-day weekend and an all-day coffee break cannot be pleasing to God. In Colossians 4:1, the masters are solemnly reminded that their Heavenly Father requires them to deal justly with their slaves.

The slave must not be moved by sentiment to feel that he will be rewarded in heaven simply because of his low estate on earth. "He that doeth wrong shall receive for the wrong which he hath done" (Col. 3:25). It is not just the high and the mighty who will be repaid for their wrongdoing but also the lowly who do wrong. God is no respecter of persons. He does not love a man because he is lowly and despise a man of high estate. God judges men by their conduct. "By their fruits ye shall know them" (Matt. 7:20).

Notes

1. Knox, *St. Paul and Church of the Gentiles,* p. 177, as quoted in Beare and MacLeod, *op. cit.,* pp. 224-25.
2. Barclay, *op. cit.,* pp. 195-96.

28. A Christian's Conduct Before the World

Colossians 4:2-6

Every Christian lives in a glass house. A Christian is the most interesting spectacle on our earth, for he makes the most staggering of claims for himself. He claims to be the child of God and an heir of heaven. As such, he is an epistle known and read of all men.

Paul said that three things must characterize a Christian's conduct before the world. He must be a man of prayer, he must walk in wisdom, and he must speak with grace.

First, he must live in the atmosphere of prayer. Prayer is the channel through which the soul rises up to God. Apart from prayer there is no sustained communion with God. Christian prayer is not the spasmodic outburst in a moment of emergency but the persistent calling on God for his guidance and blessing.

The verb *proskartereite* was used by Polybius, the historian, to depict a persistent attack during a battle. As Jacob of old, the Christian is to hold fast to God with unremitting persistence, crying, "I will not let thee go, except thou bless me" (Gen. 32:26).

Paul tells us also to watch in prayer, to be vigilant in prayer.

The word actually means be wakeful, be alert when you pray. The strong temptation is for us to allow prayer to be so routine that we drone out our familiar clichés in the drowsy moments at the close of the day. Now, there are times, to be sure, when we are so weary that all we can do is cry out in our weakness for the Holy Spirit to make intercession for us. But the normal experience is for the Christian to go to God in the strong, clear hours of the morning. Then his soul can respond mightily to the wooing of the Holy Spirit and he can vigorously intercede for the needs of mankind.

Even on the mount of transfiguration, in the high moments of revelation, the disciples fell asleep. Yet it was only when they awoke that they beheld the glory (Luke 9:32). In their natural frailty they slumbered while the Saviour poured out his soul in agony in Gethsemane. Because the flesh is weak we must give God our best and most alert moments for communion with him.

Then Paul says that you must always make thanksgiving a part of your prayer life. No man who is not aware of God's bountiful favor and blessing upon him is actually in communion with God. For the blessing of a sound mind and emotional stability; for family and friends who love us and encourage us; for the church that nurtures our souls and holds us close to Christ; and, best of all, for the Christ himself through whom God is made known to us, we should be thankful. For the high calling of God in Christ Jesus, we must be continually thankful. Paul's command is a call to conquest.

It is deeply significant that when the great apostle calls the Christian congregation at Colossae to prayer, he does not call them to pray for his comfort but for his work. He wants only the opportunity to preach Christ to others.

Many were the personal matters concerning which he might have asked this congregation to pray. He might have said, "Beseech the God of heaven to release me from this dismal dungeon that I might once more see the light of day and breathe the fresh fragrance of pure air. Claustrophobia is closing in upon me. I shall go mad if I am not soon released!"

He might have said, "Pray that God will send comfort for my thorn in the flesh. If only I could sit once more at a table with friends to partake of warm, nourishing food, for this prison fare is more unpalatable day by day."

None of this weakness comes through Paul's request. He asks only for the opportunity to serve the Lord Christ, "that God would open unto [him] a door of utterance, to speak the mystery of Christ" (Col. 4:3). Paul recognized that only God could open doors of opportunity. In 1 Corinthians 16:9, he wrote, "a wide door for effective work has opened to me" (RSV).

In Paul's instance man's extremity most surely became God's opportunity, for from his prison cell there was written a message of fadeless hope. This indicates the strength of his faith which he held fast to the end. The dungeon did not break his spirit, for his was a spirit of militant conquest.

29. A Christian's Conversation

Colossians 4:5-6

Much of the Christian world put on the black robe of sorrow when the voice of John Baillie, principal of New College of the University of Edinburgh, was silenced by death. What Longfellow wrote about Charles Sumner many of us would say about John Baillie:

Were a star quenched on high,
  For ages would its light,
Still traveling downward from the sky,
  Shine on our mortal night.

So when a great man dies,
  For years beyond our ken,
The light he leaves behind him lies
  Upon the paths of men.

He was my honored teacher whose books I long have cherished and whose lectures on the life everlasting I shall never forget. His classes were exhilarating experiences of worship. He would open his course on the doctrine of God with these words:

Gentlemen, we must remember that in discussing God we cannot talk about him without his hearing every word we say. We may be able to talk about one of our fellows, as it were, behind his back, but God is everywhere, yes, even here in this classroom. Therefore, in all of our discussions we must be aware of his infinite presence and talk about him, as it were, before his face.

Always there was a deep undertone of reverence in all of his classes. No dogmatic disparagement, no flippant disdain, nor brazen belittling was ever voiced against the great traditions which Christian hearts have cherished through many centuries.

The deep profundity of this classical scholar was often conveyed in the humblest of homilies. Once he related how a man in his last illness asked his doctor what the future life would be like. At that moment the physician heard his dog, which had followed him to the house, scratching at the door. So he told the man that his dog knew nothing of what was happening behind the door but merely wanted to be with his master. "Is it not the same with you?" he asked. "You do not know what lies behind the door, but you know your Master is there."

These two commandments of Paul to the Colossian congregation were fulfilled in the life of Dr. John Baillie. First, he walked in wisdom before the world. Second, he spoke with grace; and he, being dead, yet speaks to hundreds and through hundreds who rise up to call him blessed.

Paul spoke of the pagan world as "them that are without" (Col. 4:5). He acknowledged the stern truth that there is a wall of separation between those who follow the Saviour and those who do not. The community of the redeemed, therefore, must live in such a manner that their wisdom will impress all outsiders with the reality of God's grace. True wisdom is reflected not in one's capacity for speculation but in his superior pattern of conduct.

A Christian must make the most of every occasion by filling it with positive Christian conduct. "Redeeming the time" (v. 5), said Paul, for he thought little time remained before the return of the Master.

Fill up each hour with what will last;
Buy up the moments as they go;
The life above, when this is past,
Is the ripe fruit of life below.

HORATIUS BONAR

Every Christian must live existentially by laying hold on every favorable opportunity to demonstrate the grace of God in his conduct.

Not only must his conduct reflect the grace of God but the Christian's conversation is to be always with grace (v. 6). Charles W. Koller, in *Tents Toward the Sunrise,* tells of a great publisher who once declared:

"If you are an articulate person, you utter some thirty thousand words each day." If these words were put in print, they would amount to a fair-sized book a day. These books would, in a lifetime, fill a good-sized college library. All these books are from the same author. All reflect the life and thoughts of the author in his own words. And not a book can be taken down from the shelves. It emphasizes the fearful responsibility that goes with the gift of speech, and also the glorious privilege that is inherent in "speech seasoned with grace."[1]

Gracious Christian living involves the recognition that no man has ever been coerced into belief by harsh, critical language. He cannot be argued into the kingdom of Christ through a superior display of forensics. The overbearing pomposity of the clever and learned only drives men farther from Christ. We cannot hope to help men find Christ if we do not first love them enough to make them our friends.

When Paul said, "Let your speech be . . . seasoned with salt, that ye may know how ye ought to answer every man" (v. 6), he was no doubt recalling the words of Jesus in Mark 9:50: "Have salt in yourselves, and have peace one with another." "You are not," said the Master, "to bore your hearers with dull, insipid, sentimental generalities. There must be a certain pungency about your Christian witness." Plutarch used salt as a synonym for being witty. Nothing assists a Christian man in withstanding those who jeer at his religious faith so much as a wholesome sense of humor.

Paul felt that every Christian owed it to his Lord to develop his ability to talk intelligently and winsomely about Christ. A Christian must never be contemptuous of his fellows, thereby repelling them from Christ. A Christian must not degenerate into a puritanical scold. Christ's gracious geniality must be a part of every Christian personality. Little children never play around the doors of a scold. Neither do prodigals seek his counsel.

The winsome person whose superior serenity shines like a mellow light upon every path he walks does not have to judge others. His own innate superiority sits in judgment upon their faults and failures and speaks more eloquently than any scorching words of condemnation he might care to utter.

The grace of God enables a man to keep his temper under control when he speaks.

When a craftsman of limited training was seen often at the discussions in the Academy, a friend asked if he understood Latin, the language of the intellectuals. "No," said the craftsman, "but I can tell who is wrong in the argument." When asked how he determined this, the craftsman said: "Why, by seeing who is angry first."[2]

"Anybody can become angry—that is easy," said Aristotle; "but to be angry with the right person, and to the right degree, and at the right time, and for the right purpose, and in the right way—that is not within everybody's power and is not easy."[3]

When a Hindu woman was converted, she suffered much persecution from her husband. When the missionary asked her what she did when her husband became angry, the native said: "Well, sir, I cook his food better; when he complains, I sweep the floor cleaner; and when he speaks unkindly, I answer him mildly. I try, sir, to show him that when I became a Christian I became a better wife and a better mother."[4]

Speech that is seasoned with salt is not the doleful, depressing language of the defeatist. It must lift the heart with Christian hope.

Christ did not come to earth to tell us merely what we ought to do. He came to do something for us. He came to not merely exhort but to help. He did not come to give us good advice. That, if it were no more than that, was possibly not a thing of which we stood greatly in need for there are always plenty of people who are ready to give their advice. Advice is cheap but what Christ offered us was infinitely costly. It was the power of God unto salvation.[5]

Notes

1. Charles W. Koller, *Tents Toward the Sunrise* (Philadelphia: Judson Press, 1953), p. 67. Reprinted by permission.
2. Wallis, *A Treasury of Sermon Illustrations,* p. 16.
3. *Ibid.*
4. *Ibid.,* p. 60.
5. John Baillie, *Invitation to Pilgrimage* (New York: Charles Scribner's Sons, 1945), p. 51. By permission Charles Scribner's Sons and Oxford University Press.

30. The Gospel of Friendship

Colossians 4:7-18

Nothing is clearer to the student of the New Testament than that Christ chose to build his kingdom through forming transforming friendships among his followers. Christ's method is to stay close to men.

I looked for Christ on Madison Street
Where men went by with stumbling feet,
Where heads were bowed in the darkness there
Of gray clouds hanging low in the air.

I looked for him, a vision of white—
But gay burlesques with their crimson light
Have led my steps to a darker place
Where smoke of passion hid Christ's face.

I looked for Christ in the hidden skies,
A flaming vision to blind my eyes—
While Christ walked by with stumbling feet,
Along with the men of Madison Street.[1]

Paul brings his epistle to the Colossians to a close with many personal references to his friends in the church, men whom he says "have been a comfort unto me" (Col. 4:11). Paul trusted his friends implicitly to make his personal needs known to the Christian congregations. He chose not to write about these needs. Instead, he wrote, "Tychicus [beloved brother, faithful minister, and my fellow slave in Christ] will tell you all about my affairs" (Col. 4:7, RSV).

Tychicus was the personal envoy of Paul and the bearer of the circular letter which we know as Ephesians to the various churches. His home was in the Roman province of Asia. He probably had been entrusted with the responsibility of bearing the offering of the Gentile congregations of Macedonia and Achaia to the mother church for the relief of the poor (Rom. 15:25-26).

Onesimus was a native of Colossae and is called also "a faithful and beloved brother" (v. 9). He was the runaway slave whose story is recorded in Philemon. Calvin insisted that this could not be the same Onesimus because he was a fugitive and a thief. Yet, this background stands as strong evidence of the transforming grace of God. He has been forgiven now and is under no reproach. His past has been forgotten.

Aristarchus was a native of Thessalonica and a Jew by birth. He is called the "fellow captive," which meant he willingly shared the bondage of all believers in Christ. The conquering Christ had laid claim to him.

Three times Aristarchus stood out in the New Testament. The first was during the riot in Ephesus in the Temple of Diana when he was captured by the mob (Acts 19:29). The second was when Paul set sail as a prisoner for Rome (Acts 27:2). Finally, he was found with Paul in Rome. It seemed that he was the stalwart friend in the time of crisis, a man upon whom Paul could count in his hour of need, a strong defender of the faith, always on hand when he was needed.

Then Paul mentions Mark, the cousin of Barnabas, who deserted Paul and Barnabas on their first missionary journey. Paul was so distressed that he refused to take him on his second missionary journey. Clearly, however, the intervening years have healed the rift. Mark now is the quitter who quit quitting. He is with Paul in his last imprisonment. Paul, therefore, instructs the congregation to welcome Mark. This may mean that the churches now were reluctant to receive him because of his previous desertion.

The next man mentioned is Jesus, who was called Justus (v. 11). Many a Jewish boy was named Jesus. Our blessed Lord's humility is reflected in his choice of a very common name for himself.

Only three of the Jewish Christian party stood by Paul. Even at the end of his life the Jewish party opposed him.

Epaphras was the founder of the Colossian church and the overseer also of the churches in Laodicea and Hierapolis, on either side of the Lycus River. He was supremely the good pastor who labored fervently for his flock (v. 12).

The verb which was originally used to describe striving for the prize in games of track and field also denoted the supreme struggles of life. It is used here to describe intercessory prayer as strenuous physical exertion.

Paul said, "Epaphras has heavy toil on your behalf." He was referring to the earnest outpouring of his soul in prayer. The object of his prayers was that the Colossians might "stand mature and fully assured in all the will of God" (v. 12, RSV). This good pastor saw the constant peril of his people who were under the pressure of false teachers and, therefore, prayed that they might "stand"; that is, that they might be firm and not waver in the face of heavy pressure.

He reminded them that the will of God was the sphere in which the Christian life must be lived. It was the very breath of life to them.

Then Paul mentions Luke whom he has passed on to the Christian church with the imperishable encomium, "Luke, the beloved physician" (v. 14). In the same simple sentence he mentions

Demas. Here we have, side by side, representatives of the whitest fidelity and the blackest apostasy.

Concerning Demas, Paul says nothing here at all. He is the man who refused to accept the transforming friendship of Christ and of Paul. As the apostolic band included Judas, the fellow laborers of Paul included Demas (Phil. 24). In 2 Timothy 4:10, it is recorded that "Demas hath forsaken me, having loved this present world."

Not all the friends of Paul were loyal. It required supreme courage to declare friendship with a man whose life current ran counter to the Roman world and who, therefore, was a prisoner of Rome. The declaration that Demas loved this present world may indicate the extreme danger in which every Christian lived and the necessity of laying down his life for the Lord Christ and thereby giving up this present world to pass with his Master into eternity.

Nympha was probably an important matron in Colossae. The church of the brothers (v. 15, RSV) met in her house. That which was important about the early church was not the building but the brotherhood. The church had no roof over her head in the first three hundred years of her history; yet these were the years when she grew most rapidly. We should not forget the church which worshiped in the houses of Aquila and Prisca in Rome and Ephesus (Rom. 16:5, 1 Cor. 16:19) and of Philemon (v. 2.) In early Christian days the church and the home were closely bound together.

The Laodicean letter which Paul mentions was probably destroyed before Paul's letters were collected. It is not likely that we have all of Paul's letters, for he surely wrote more than thirteen letters in fifteen years. Archippus had received a task from someone else, perhaps from Epaphras (v. 17). We cannot know for certain. The entire congregation is called upon to share the responsibility for fulfilling his task.

Paul does not close his letter with a bland assurance of brighter days but with the grim reminder of his bonds. Perhaps the impress of the chain was left on the papyri on which he wrote. He makes no sentimental appeal for sympathy but encourages the Colossians to endure hardship as he has done. His suffering gives him authority to challenge his fellow servants not to be ashamed to suffer for the Saviour.

No sensitive soul could take this letter lightly, for it was written by one who had passed through great anguish and was, therefore, serving Christ at great cost.

This epistle is brought to a close, as Paul closes all of his epistles, with the certain reminder that it is by the grace of God that the gospel has come to us; in his grace we are sustained and by his grace we shall one day overcome every adversary (v. 18). This epistle began with a prayer for grace and now it ends with the same prayer.

Colossae was probably the least important of the early churches. It was soon to vanish. Yet, to this small church Paul wrote the letter in which the doctrine of Christ reached its zenith.

E. Stanley Jones once stood in a little village in India and saw an artist watching the magnificent sunset on the monsoon clouds and heard him exclaim, "What a wonderful sunset for such a little place!" So the Christ who is enthroned in suns and stars came to Colossae and still comes to the lowliest places as the shepherd of the lowliest souls and the highest stars.

Notes

1. Raymond Kresensky, "I Looked for Christ," quoted in Charles L. Wallis, ed. *Worship Resources for the Christian Year* (New York: Harper & Brothers, 1954), p. 399. By permission Harper & Brothers.